Space Grid Structures
Skeletal Frameworks and Stressed-Skin Systems

Space Grid Structures
Skeletal Frameworks and Stressed-Skin Systems

by John Borrego

The MIT Press Massachusetts Institute of Technology Cambridge, Massachusetts, and London, England

Copyright © 1968 by
The Massachusetts Institute of Technology

Second Printing, November 1969
Third Printing, September 1972
Fourth Printing, April 1977

Set in Linotype Helvetica by P. and M. Typesetting, Inc.
and printed and bound in the United States of America
by The Halliday Lithograph Corp.

ISBN 262 52009 5 (paperback)

Library of Congress catalog card number: 67-27342

FOR TEDDI

Contents

Introduction

This book is intended to be an exchange of information about what has been done recently in the development of flat space grid structures. Most of the projects covered attempt to utilize recent technology to develop structural systems that will cope with the economic and organizational trends of society. In an age of standardization and prefabrication, their simplicity of manufacture, ease of transportation and speed of erection are sufficient recommendation. Even more important, the ratio of weight to area covered can be greatly reduced through their use, and they allow the construction of long-span structures with a greatly reduced number of intermediate columns. These systems are capable of accommodating a large amount of mechanical services within their structural depth. These flat double-layer space grids consist of two-plane parallel grids that are connected by vertical and inclined "web" members in such a way that external loads are rapidly distributed omnidirectionally among numerous bars. Even under the pressures of a heavily concentrated load, members at a considerable distance share the load, so that the network exhibits a remarkably even stress distribution.

The projects in Part I present a cross section of the possibilities in flat double-layer space grid structures. These include two-, three-, and four-way systems. The projects cover various geometries, fabrication techniques, joint solutions, and the material possibilities in steel, aluminum, plastic, concrete, wood, etc., that have been proposed for this kind of structural system.

Part II is concerned with stressed-skin space grids, fabricated from triangular, orthagonal, and hexagonal pyramids. Some are constructed from flat sheets and bent plates as opposed to prefabricated pyramids or some other three-dimensional form.

Part III is an index to the space grid geometries, some of which are graphically described. The networks are shown in isometric and plan. In addition, the top grid, the interconnecting vertical and diagonal web members, and the bottom grid are diagramed. An extensive bibliography is included.

Cambridge, Massachusetts
September 1967

John Borrego

Acknowledgments
For their contribution the author is greatly indebted to:
Department of Architecture, School of Architecture and
Planning, Massachusetts Institute of Technology; Dean
Lawrence Anderson; Professor Horacio Caminos; Professor
Eduardo Catalano (thesis adviser); Professor Waclaw
Zalewski; Mr. Leon Groisser; Professor Z. S. Makowski,
Head of the Department of Civil Engineering, University
of Surrey, London, England; and the individuals and
firms who allowed me to present their work here.

2

Flat skeletal double-layer space grids are a three-dimensional development of the grid. These systems consist of two parallel-plane grids interconnected by vertical and inclined web members in which external loads are spread omnidirectionally among many bars in three or more directions in space. They are well suited for structures that may be subjected to heavy concentrated loads. The axially loaded members have an even stress distribution on their cross-sectional area because of the elimination of bending moments.[1] Because they are highly indeterminate structures with the ability to distribute concentrated loads evenly throughout the rest of the space grid, the buckling of a member under a concentrated load does not lead to the collapse of the entire structure.

From the point of view of geometry, the space grid can be visualized as a three-dimensional development of the grid. The single-layer grid has only 3 polygons—the triangle, square, hexagon—which allow a complete equipartitioning or filling of a plane. In dealing with space structures, we have to think of the unit cell as a three-dimensional unit filling space. In the analysis of the cell, the undeformability can be verified by the degree of determinacy.[2] In a space grid, each joint requires three bars to maintain equilibrium unless all the forces acting on the joint lie in one plane, in which case only two bars are needed. Therefore the number of bars plus the number of components of the reactions must be equal to three times the number of joints at which the forces are non-coplanar plus two times the number of joints at which the forces are coplaner, or

$$n = 3j_1 + 2j_2 - r$$

where n = number of members for internal stability

j_1 = joints with non-coplanar forces,
j_2 = joints with coplanar forces,
r = number of components at the supports.

Because in most cells under consideration all joints have non-coplanar forces, and in general there will be six reactive forces, we can write this formula for the stability of space frames:

$$n = 3j - 6$$

Structures in which the members are subjected to shear and bending moments as well as axial stresses cannot, of course, be investigated in this way.

There are four types of top-grid to bottom-grid relationships in double-layer space grid geometries. These are

DIRECT GRIDS. Two parallel grids similar in design, with one layer directly over the top of the other; thus both grids are directionally the same. Upper and lower grids are interconnected by bracing.
OFFSET GRIDS. Two parallel grids similar in design with one grid offset from the other (in plan) but remaining directionally the same. The upper and lower grids are interconnected by bracing.
DIFFERENTIAL GRID. Two parallel grids that may be of different design and are therefore directionally different but are chosen to co-ordinate and form a regular pattern. Upper and lower grids are interconnected by bracing.
LATTICE GRIDS. The upper and lower members are braced to form a girder prior to erection; they are generally factory-fabricated assemblies. In this type of assembly the upper and lower members are placed close together and when joined by bracing may be considered as a stiffened single member. The finished grid may be considered a stiffened single-layer grid. In all other respects it is similar in appearance to a direct grid. These are further discussed and defined in Section III, Space Grid Geometries.

In multistory buildings the space between the top and bottom grids is ample for the installation and maintenance of the mechanical and electrical services (heating, cooling, and ventilating). This capacity is essential in buildings whose use requires a completely flexible space, unencumbered by structural, mechanical, or major circulation systems. This is of special importance in buildings in which the requirements of the tenants may change over time. The flat space grid can provide a large, column-free roof system with a depth of about 1/20 to 1/25 or a floor system of 60–80 × 60–80 ft sq with a depth of 1/16 to 1/20 of the span or 4–5' deep. This internal space can house and circulate the essential building services.

When confronted with the requirements of a large amount of mechanical services, of maximum span, and a horizontal floor with a minimum of material, the space grid system on a square module which integrates the main vertical compression members into the geometry and which utilizes the large amount of material in floor systems structurally (thus reducing the level of main stress and therefore of deflection) seems to be a logical solution.

[1] Dr. Z. S. Makowski, "Double-Layer Grid Structures," *Architectural Association Journal*, March 1961. p. 218.

[2] R. Le Ricolais, "Grids and Space Frames—an investigation on structures." A Graduate Report, University of Michigan pp. 16–24.

Space grids may behave as a grillage or a slab.[3] Offset and differential space grids, which behave as a slab, provide stiffness even as pin-jointed systems whose members can be axially loaded with little bending, just as in a plane truss. The behavior of the space grid can be compared with that of a reinforced concrete slab except that in the space grid the forces must follow the path provided by the members instead of spreading as they would in a slab. This type of space frame can resist torsion or twisting moments through axial member loading alone; it is stiffer than the grillage type of space frame. Lattice and direct space grids function like grillages with top chords and bottom chords, with vertical and inclined web members contained in a plane normal to the flat roof or floor system. No matter how many directions there are in such vertical trusses, the result is still a grillage of plane trusses and must be analyzed and designed accordingly. The actual force distribution of both types, slab or grillage, depends primarily on the nature of the supports. Several types of supporting structure along with the induced behavior on the space grids will be discussed. The support locations significantly affect the structural efficiency of the space grids, so that those systems with symmetry about two or three axes are preferable. Systems with cantilevers have less chord material, less over-all material, but do not change the size of web members. The space grid can transfer its loads to the supporting structure in the following ways: The structure may be made continuous with the space grid, or the junction between the space grid and the vertical support may be a pin connection. Supports are seldom made continuous with the space grid in order to reduce deflections because space grids are deep and many times stiffer than their vertical supports. The lateral loads can be resisted by vertical supports with fixed bases. The problem of support perimeter can be achieved, regardless of continuity, by shearhead-type connectors at the junction of the vertical support and the space grid. Some basic supporting conditions for space grids follow. I have limited myself to an offset, orthogonal, two-way double-layer space grid. The square bay has spans of 12 modules and cantilevers of 3 modules.

1. A column-supported space grid behaves like a flat plate in concrete. The trusses between the columns serve in place of beams and receive loads from the rest of the grid in full. Because of this behavior, beams were introduced which transfer the loads from the grid to the columns. Because of the concentration of forces at supports, these beams or shearheads can also be used at point supports as well as along continuously supported conditions.

2. If the space grid is supported on parallel walls, the action of the system is primarily unidirectional as in a one-way slab with the forces traveling the most direct path to the support. Practically, the system can be treated as a system of parallel triangular trusses, with the members on the top and bottom grid parallel to the supports, which brace the structure and make it more rigid. When the space grid must sustain concentrated loads, thus trussing tends to equalize deflections and spread the concentrated loads to the adjoining trusses.

3. A space grid supported by peripheral walls or a system of exterior and interior walls behaves like a two-way concrete slab. The load being carried is distributed between two or more truss systems with separate chord systems and common webs.

The following plans and sections illustrate these and other supporting conditions that are a combination of the three conditions just described.

   Row 1. Simple column and wall combinations
   Row 2. Column and wall combinations with beams (shear-heads) to distribute the forces over a larger area, therefore reduce the unit stress of the element at the support area.
   Row 3. These are all columnar systems with beams that receive loads from the rest of the grid.

The flat space grid has a concentration of forces where it is vertically supported. If a space structure were point-supported, the members immediately adjacent to the head of the column would be overstressed. Pinned and continuous vertical supports can be designed to support space grids. If one or the other of these is not possible, then some other means must be found to stabilize the space structure laterally.

The following plans and sections illustrate some of the basic *one-point, four-point stud, four-point pyramidal,* and *nine-point pyramidal* supporting conditions, according to the number of contact points with the main space frame. These could be used for an offset, orthogonal, two-way double-layer space grid. The shaded area shows the tributary area of the supporting condition. It is possible to combine the three supporting types, i.e., peripheral or parallel supports with one or more column supports. The other geometries and their supporting conditions can only be suggested here as they are infinite.

In space grids, the module or unit dimensions are dictated by many factors, i.e., the height module (span), member shape, building planning module, joint cost (the larger the tributary feet to the joint, the more economical), ratio of bending stress to direct stress, ratio of the horizontal spacing to the depth of the structure.[4] The joint fabrication, to be economical, must consider the type and size of the members, their geometric relationships, connecting techniques (bolting, welding, special connectors), and desired appearance. Tubular members, structural tees, angle, and wide flange members each imply a connection discipline.

[3]D. T. Wright, "Space Frames," *RAIC/LTRAC Journal*, June 1964, (Reprint, p. 1).

[4]Kenneth C. Nashlund, "Design Considerations for Horizontal Space Frames," *Architectural Record*, August 1964 pp. 152–155.

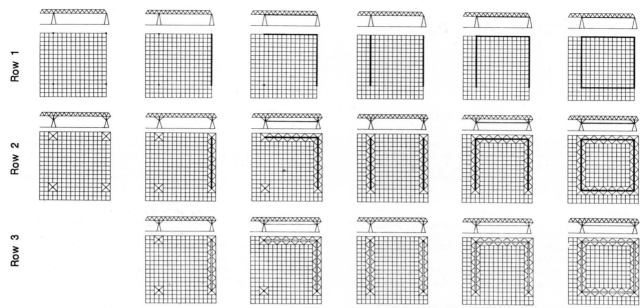

For instance, the advantage of the welding connection is that it eliminates extra connection material and connection devices—some tubular members need a joint piece to obtain enough weld to develop the member stress. On the other hand, bolted connections require joint material or assemblies that extend out of the members, increasing the cost of the connection.

A space grid system, to be economical, should permit maximum shop fabrication of easily manufactured shapes that allow variations in length, strength of elements, and universal joints; a reliable structural analysis must also be developed. Ease and economy of transportation of subassembly units and ease of site erection are important factors; the number of units and connections should be minimized.

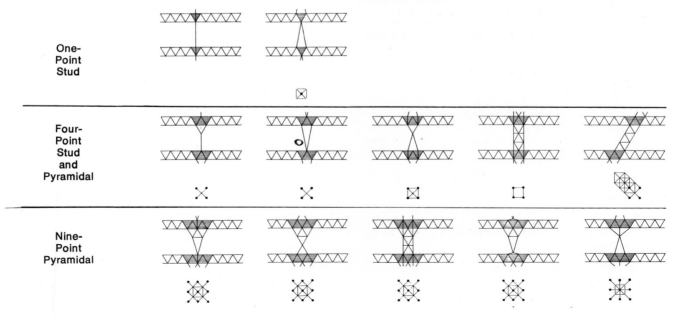

A Space Frame Structure

Project by Horacio Caminos and Charles Howard Kahn, 1961. This space frame structure was proposed for 3 or 4 story multipurpose buildings for offices, laboratories, and small factories. The perspective describes schematically the functional requirements of such buildings.

Building Units

In designing the building it is proper to consider the problem of the expansion joints from the initial stages of the design because in a large building the expansion joints divide the structure into independent units.

In the present case different building units have been proposed. Their dimensions have been determined by the following factors:

a. Maximum unit dimension based on thermal expansion limitations
b. Maximum utilization of the space
c. Width of circulation
d. Flexibility, simplicity, and variety of combinations
e. Structural efficiency of the two-way system adopted
f. Type of columns

Proposed Systems of Construction

Two different methods of construction are outlined. It is plain that the methods suggested in the following paragraphs demand a careful study and only experience with full-scale prototypes can provide adequate information on the practical difficulties involved with either of the methods proposed.

a. 1. Space frame elements produced in factory
   2. Space frame floors assembled on the site
   3. Concrete slab poured
   4. Space frames lifted into position using jacks
   5. Columns placed and attached
b. 1. Space frame elements produced in factory
   2. Space frames assembled at the final level as in standard construction and supported with a minimum of scaffolding
   3. The concrete slab is poured
   4. After curing of concrete, scaffolding is removed

Typical Element

The element has the following components, all in aluminum:
1. Form panel (pressed)
2. Top chord channel with integral shear lugs (extruded)
3. Top joint (cast)
4. Diagonal tube (extruded)
5. Bottom chord tube (extruded)
6. Bottom joint (cast)

The top surface of the element is a structural slab in reinforced concrete with a 6 x 6 No. 4 standard steel wire fabric. For speed and ease of erection, bolted connections have been minimized, and only one has been provided in each element. All other connections are snap-in and mechanical locking joints.

Fireproofing is not indicated but should be provided on the 5' x 5' ceiling panels. These panels should be attached to the bottom of the structure in such a manner that they can be removed easily for the installation of ducts and pipes and panels of varying function.

The ceiling panels will contain lighting and air conditioning fixtures as well as fireproofing and acoustical treatment.

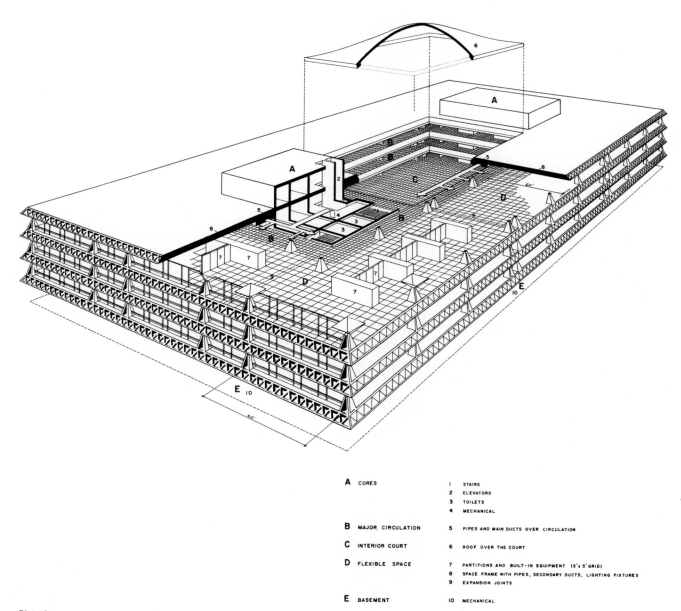

Plate 1
Typical building describing schematically the functional requirements.

A	CORES	I	STAIRS
		2	ELEVATORS
		3	TOILETS
		4	MECHANICAL
B	MAJOR CIRCULATION	5	PIPES AND MAIN DUCTS OVER CIRCULATION
C	INTERIOR COURT	6	ROOF OVER THE COURT
D	FLEXIBLE SPACE	7	PARTITIONS AND BUILT-IN EQUIPMENT (5'x 5' GRID)
		8	SPACE FRAME WITH PIPES, SECONDARY DUCTS, LIGHTING FIXTURES
		9	EXPANSION JOINTS
E	BASEMENT	10	MECHANICAL

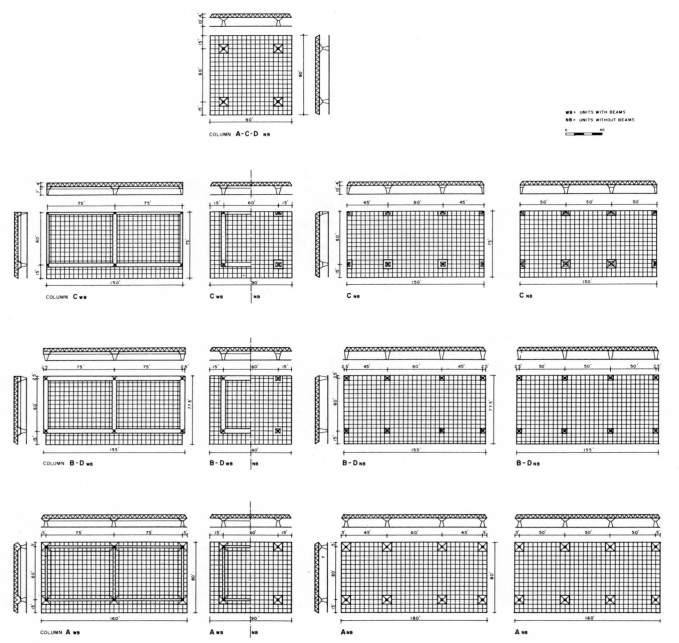

WB = UNITS WITH BEAMS
NB = UNITS WITHOUT BEAMS

COLUMN A-C-D NB

COLUMN C WB   C WB | NB   C NB   C NB

COLUMN B-D WB   B-D WB | NB   B-D NB   B-D NB

COLUMN A WB   A WB | NB   A NB   A NB

Plate 2
The building units shown on this sheet have been composed on
a 5′ × 5′ structural grid.

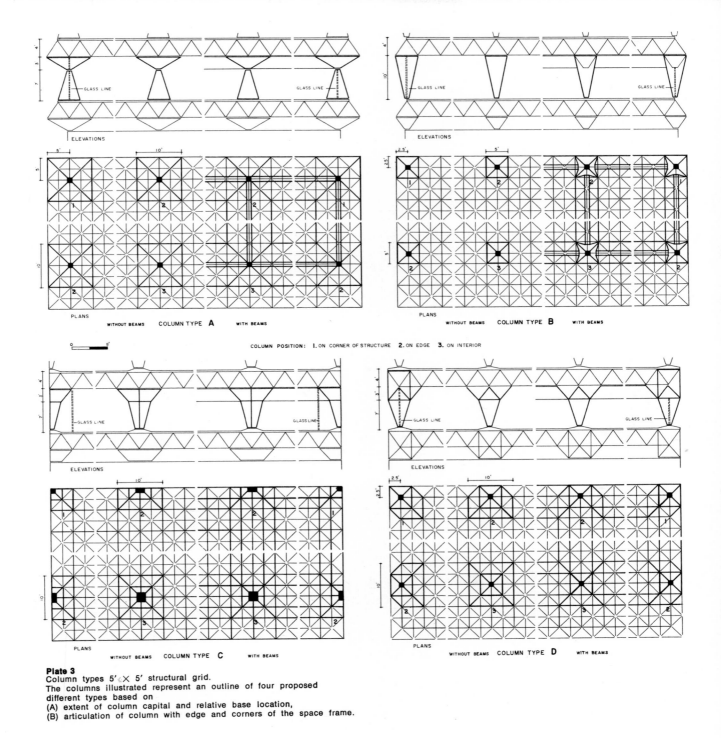

ELEVATIONS

PLANS

WITHOUT BEAMS   COLUMN TYPE **A**   WITH BEAMS

ELEVATIONS

PLANS

WITHOUT BEAMS   COLUMN TYPE **B**   WITH BEAMS

COLUMN POSITION: **1.** ON CORNER OF STRUCTURE   **2.** ON EDGE   **3.** ON INTERIOR

ELEVATIONS

PLANS

WITHOUT BEAMS   COLUMN TYPE **C**   WITH BEAMS

ELEVATIONS

PLANS

WITHOUT BEAMS   COLUMN TYPE **D**   WITH BEAMS

Plate 3
Column types 5′ × 5′ structural grid.
The columns illustrated represent an outline of four proposed
different types based on
(A) extent of column capital and relative base location,
(B) articulation of column with edge and corners of the space frame.

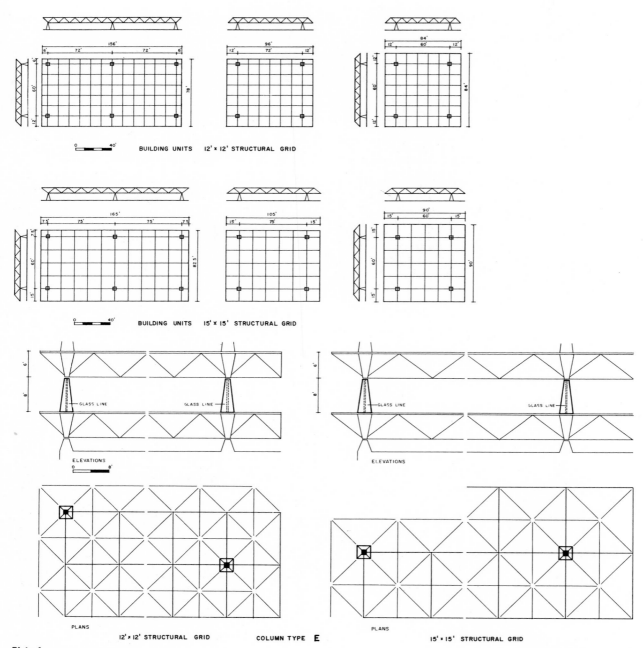

BUILDING UNITS   12' × 12' STRUCTURAL GRID

BUILDING UNITS   15' × 15' STRUCTURAL GRID

ELEVATIONS

ELEVATIONS

PLANS

PLANS

12' × 12' STRUCTURAL GRID   COLUMN TYPE **E**

15' × 15' STRUCTURAL GRID

Plate 4
Building units—column types.
The proposed building units shown on this sheet are arranged
in two different structural grids: 12′ × 12′ and 15′ × 15′

10

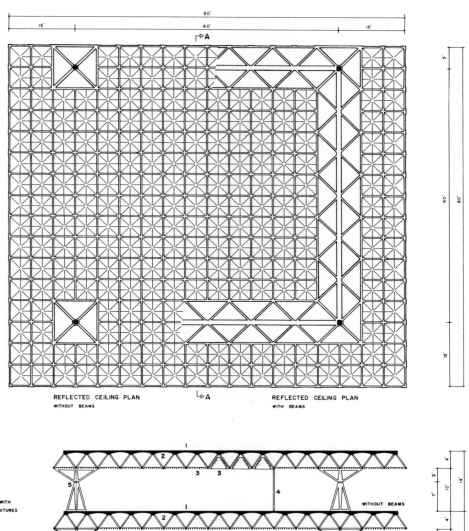

REFLECTED CEILING PLAN
WITHOUT BEAMS

REFLECTED CEILING PLAN
WITH BEAMS

1   CONCRETE SLAB

2   SPACE FOR DUCTS

3   TWO TYPES OF CEILING PANELS WITH
      LIGHTING AND AIR CONDITIONING FIXTURES

4   PARTITIONS UNDER GRID 5' X 5'

5   GLASS LINE

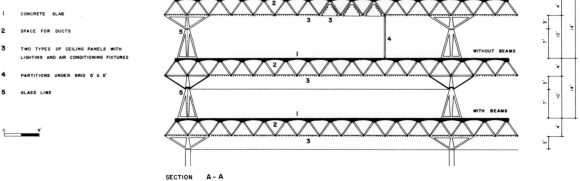

WITHOUT BEAMS

WITH BEAMS

SECTION   A - A

Plate 5
A typical unit 5′ × 5′ structural grid.

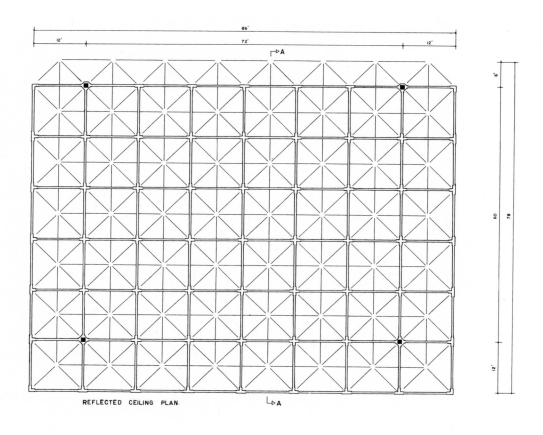

REFLECTED CEILING PLAN.

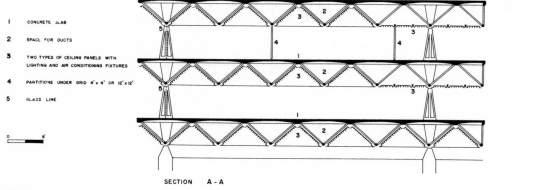

1   CONCRETE SLAB

2   SPACE FOR DUCTS

3   TWO TYPES OF CEILING PANELS WITH
    LIGHTING AND AIR CONDITIONING FIXTURES

4   PARTITIONS UNDER GRID 4' x 4' OR 12' x 12'

5   GLASS LINE

SECTION   A - A

Plate 6
A typical unit 12′ × 12′ structural grid.

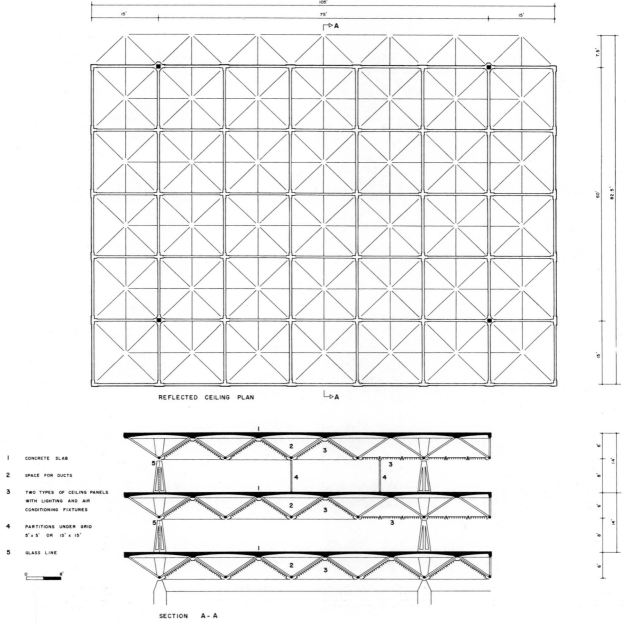

REFLECTED CEILING PLAN

SECTION A - A

1   CONCRETE SLAB

2   SPACE FOR DUCTS

3   TWO TYPES OF CEILING PANELS
    WITH LIGHTING AND AIR
    CONDITIONING FIXTURES

4   PARTITIONS UNDER GRID
    5' x 5'   OR   15' x 15'

5   GLASS LINE

Plate 7
A typical unit 15′ × 15′ structural grid.

13

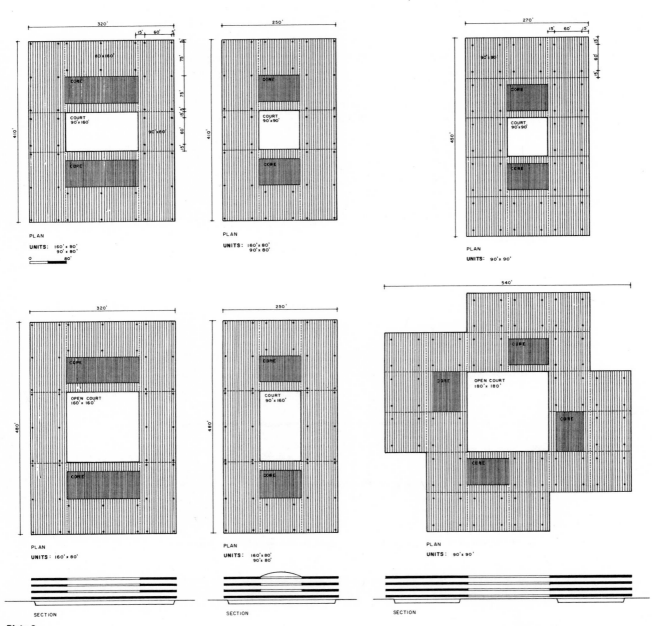

Plate 8
Examples of building variations.

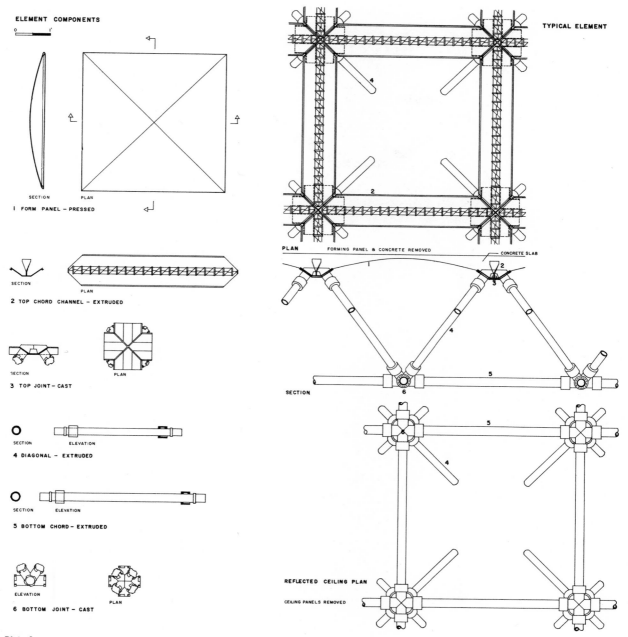

ELEMENT COMPONENTS

0   1'

SECTION   PLAN

1 FORM PANEL — PRESSED

SECTION

PLAN

2 TOP CHORD CHANNEL — EXTRUDED

SECTION   PLAN

3 TOP JOINT — CAST

SECTION   ELEVATION

4 DIAGONAL — EXTRUDED

SECTION   ELEVATION

5 BOTTOM CHORD — EXTRUDED

ELEVATION   PLAN

6 BOTTOM JOINT — CAST

TYPICAL ELEMENT

PLAN   FORMING PANEL & CONCRETE REMOVED

CONCRETE SLAB

SECTION

REFLECTED CEILING PLAN

CEILING PANELS REMOVED

Plate 9
Typical element. This sheet shows the space frame element as assembled
and its component parts. Dimensions: Modular grid—5' × 5';
total height—4'.

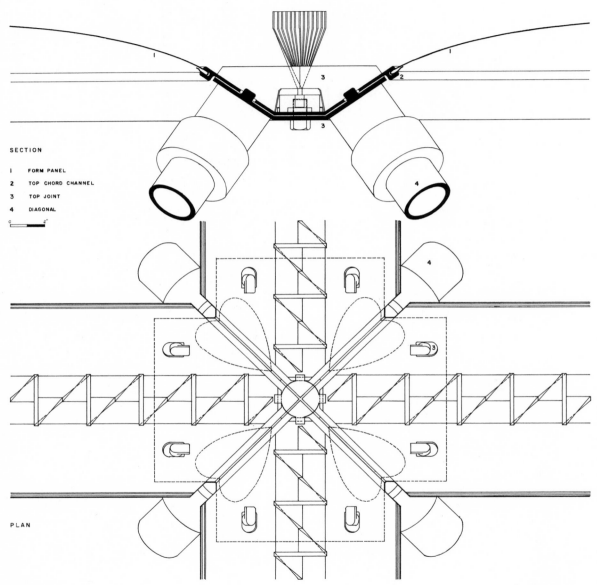

SECTION

1   FORM PANEL

2   TOP CHORD CHANNEL

3   TOP JOINT

4   DIAGONAL

PLAN

Plate 10
Top joint details.

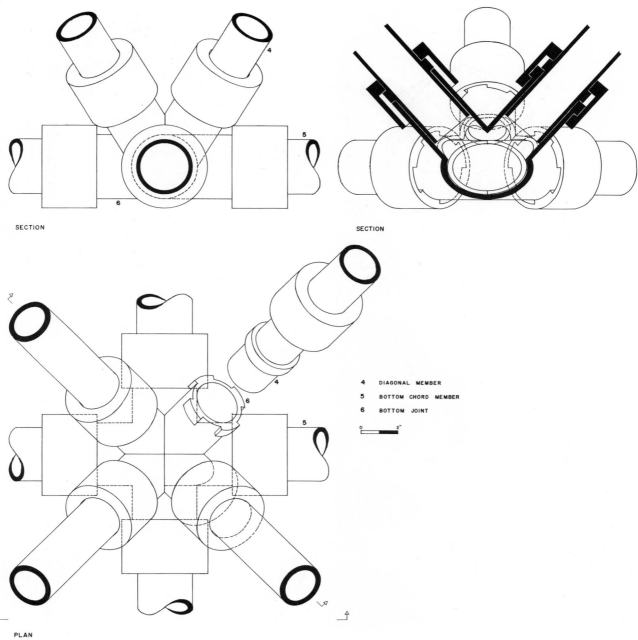

SECTION

SECTION

4 DIAGONAL MEMBER

5 BOTTOM CHORD MEMBER

6 BOTTOM JOINT

0 _____ 2"

PLAN

Plate 11
Bottom joint details.

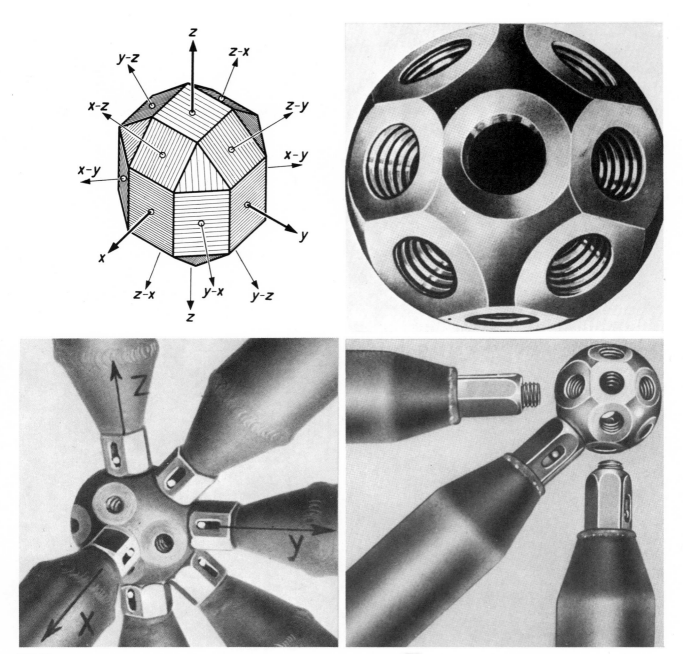

Plate 12
MERO-TRIGONAL system by Dr. Ing. Max Mengeringhausen. 1. Definition of the joint geometry, a lesser rhombicuboctahedron. 2. The node transformed into reality is a threaded steel ball responding to the geometrical requirements. 3. The three principal axes of the node (x, y, z,) enable up to 8 members to be connected in any of the three planes at angles of 45°. 4. The MERO members are thin-walled steel tubes with a coupling device, a retractable bolt that screws into the threaded ball.

Plate 13
1. MERO Connection. 2. Geometric possibilities of the MERO space grid system.

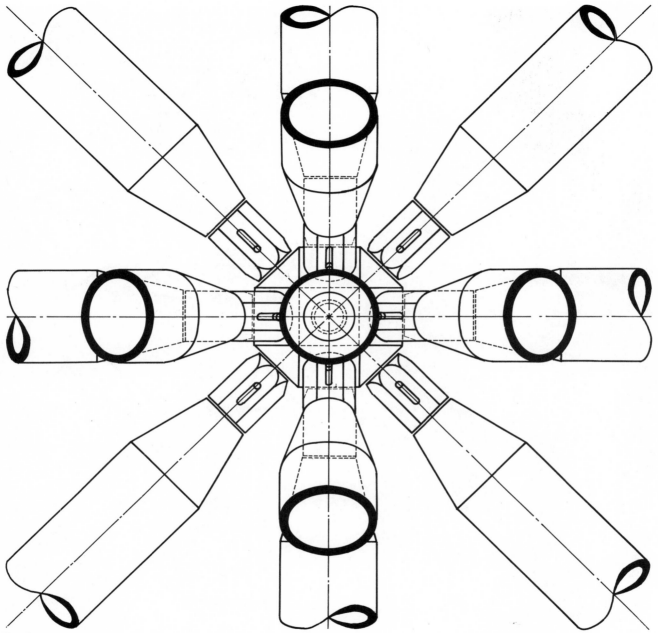

Plate 14
Plan of joint showing all possible members coming into the node.
The guide pins inside slot hold the bolts in during transport.

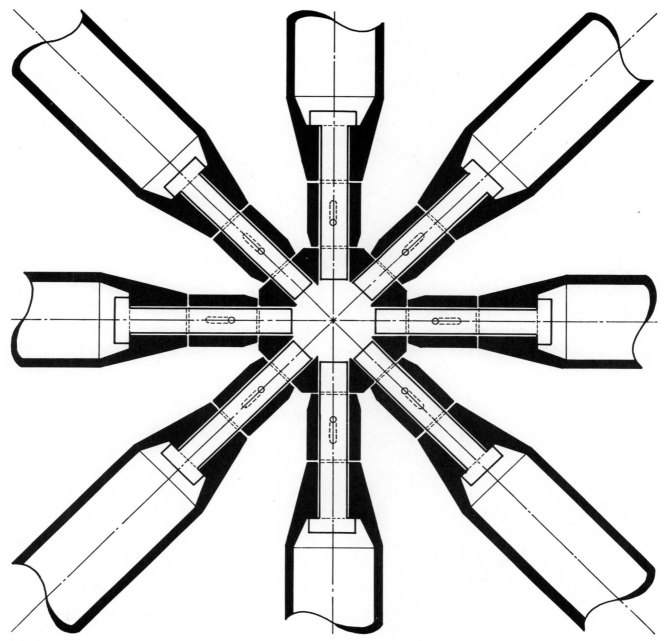

Plate 15
Horizontal section through the MERO globe and struts showing the retractable bolts.

21

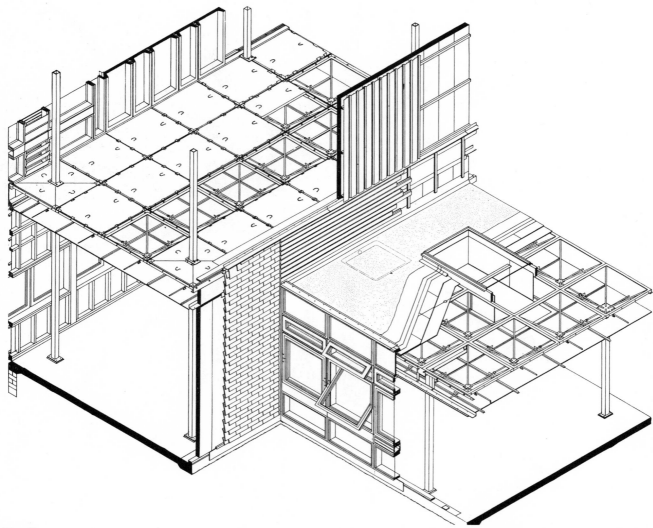

Plate 16
The NENK method of construction was developed by Roger Walters and Ralph Iredale, both from the Directorate General of Research and Development, Ministry of Public Buildings and Works, London, England. It is intended to satisfy the requirements of a wide range of buildings, not exceeding at this stage of development 4 stories in height. The structural frame consists of a double-layer flat grid space frame for both floor and roof decks. It clear spans 40′ with 60 lb per sq ft floor loads and spans 88′ with 15-lb roof loads. The isometric shows the assembly of NENK components.

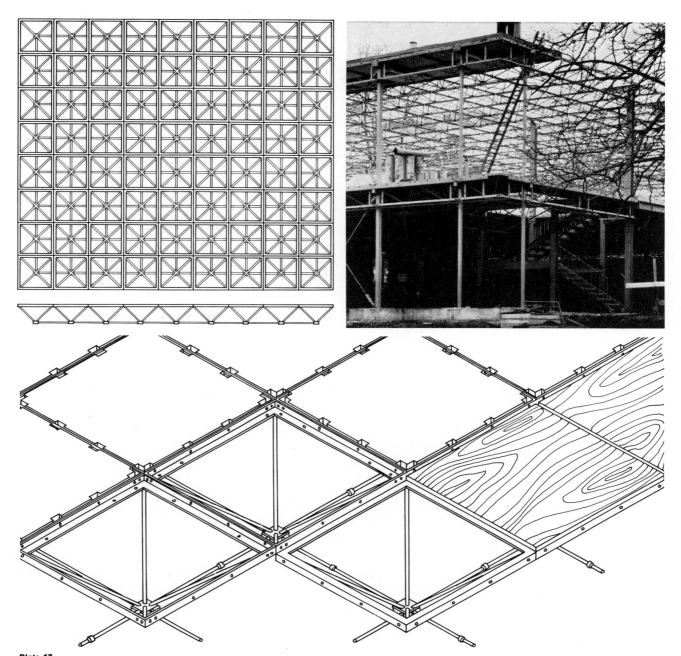

Plate 17
1. Plan and section of the structural grid. 2. The structural frame
with the roof decking being fixed in position. 3. The space frame
is formed of prefabricated steel pyramids, 4' sq in plan and 2'
deep finished floor to ceiling. The pyramids are welded frames made
from mild steel angles with rod or steel tube diagonals connecting
to steel bosses.

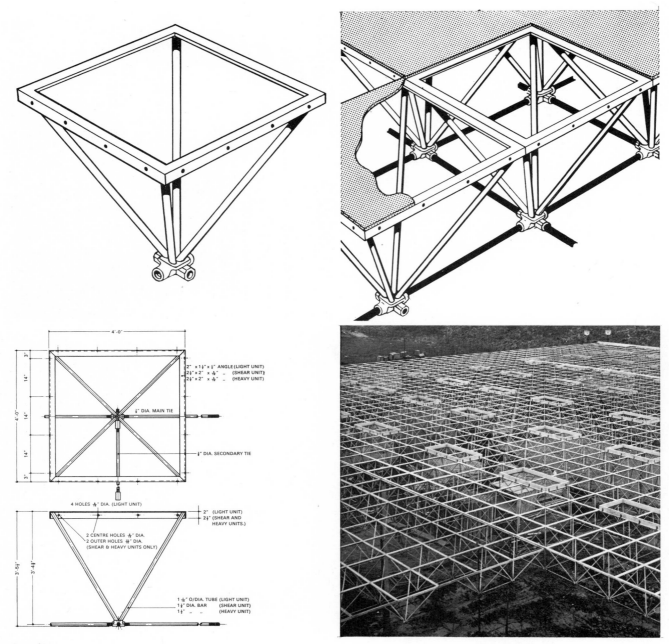

Plate 18

The SPACE DECK Structural System is fabricated and patented by Denings of Chard Ltd., England. The SPACE DECK standard roof consists of: 1.—2. an open square-based pyramid. Four tubular diagonals join the corners of the 4'-sq angle section to a boss (or apex piece), which in turn is threaded to take four adjustable tie bars. 3. Dimensions of a typical pyramid module. 4. View of assembled

SPACE DECK System. The standard SPACE DECK roof units, made to a 4' × 4' plan module, are 3'—6" deep. The lightness of these units allows up to a 72' one-way clear span, or a 124' × 124' two-way span, or can be supported on columns at varying centers with an economical arrangement being 40' × 40'.

Labels on drawing 3 (dimensioned module):

4'-0"
3"
14"
4'-0"
14"
14"
14"
3"

2" × 1½" × ¼" ANGLE (LIGHT UNIT)
2½" × 2" × 3/16" " (SHEAR UNIT)
2½" × 2" × ¼" " (HEAVY UNIT)

¾" DIA. MAIN TIE

½" DIA. SECONDARY TIE

4 HOLES 7/16 DIA. (LIGHT UNIT)

2" (LIGHT UNIT)
2½" (SHEAR AND HEAVY UNITS.)

2 CENTRE HOLES 7/16 DIA.
2 OUTER HOLES 11/16 DIA.
(SHEAR & HEAVY UNITS ONLY)

3'-5½"
3'-4½"

1¼" O/DIA. TUBE (LIGHT UNIT)
1¼" DIA. BAR (SHEAR UNIT)
1½" " (HEAVY UNIT)

Plate 19
1. The prefabricated pyramids shown nested for shipping; up to 7,000 sq ft of roofing can be placed on one lorry. 2.—3. Pyramids being mounted into beams, which are then turned over. 4. Sections being lifted into position; entire bays can also be lifted into position.
5. Completed framework. 6. View of supports.

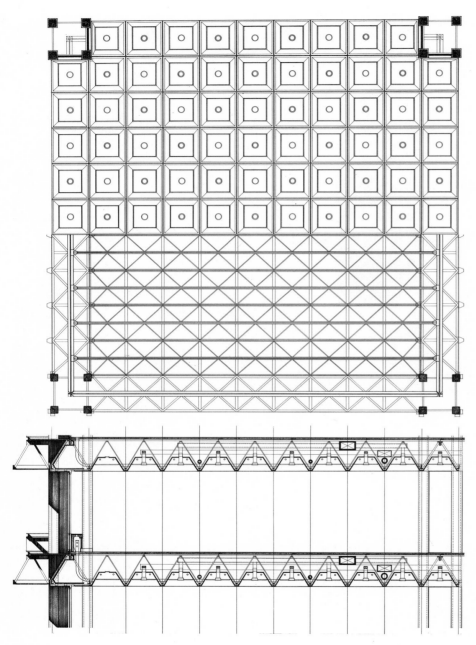

Plate 20
Project by D. K. Davies, M.Arch. Thesis at the Massachusetts
Institute of Technology School of Architecture and Planning under
Eduardo Catalano and Waclaw Zalewski, 1965. A building for a laboratory
research center, utilizing a space frame structure. 1. Plan of a
structural bay on a 5' module showing columns, beams and infill units,
also a partial plan of the reflected ceiling. The structure is made
up of large bar joists, interconnected by the lower chords and upper
floor slab into a two-way space grid. 2. Section of a typical edge
bay showing how the mechanical is integrated within the structural height.

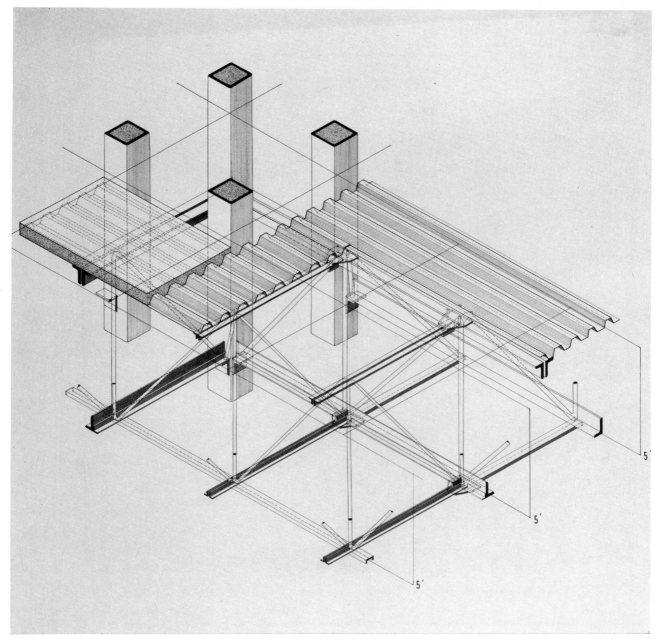

5'

5'

5'

Plate 21
Axonometric of the column construction showing how the space
grid structure is formed and the details of its fabrication.

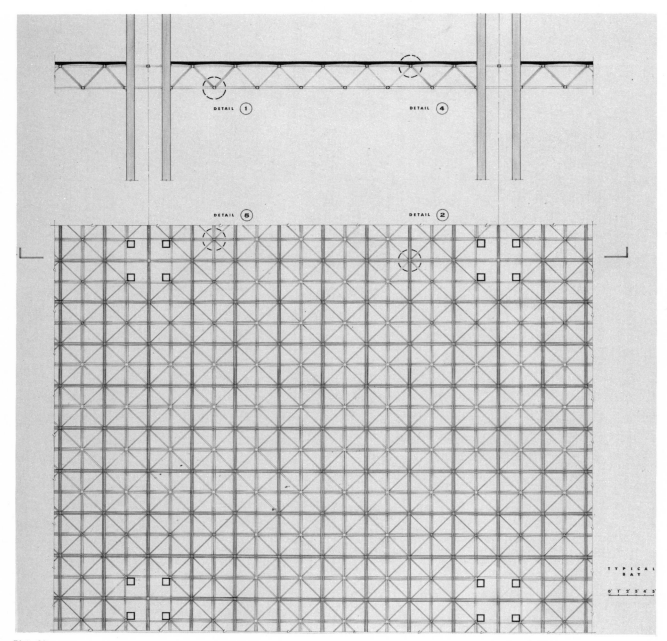

Plate 22
Project by Robert Taylor, M.Arch. Thesis at the Massachusetts
Institute of Technology School of Architecture and Planning under
Eduardo Catalano, 1965. A space grid system made from either angle,
channel, or tee components, on a 5' module. The column spacing
is 50' × 50'.

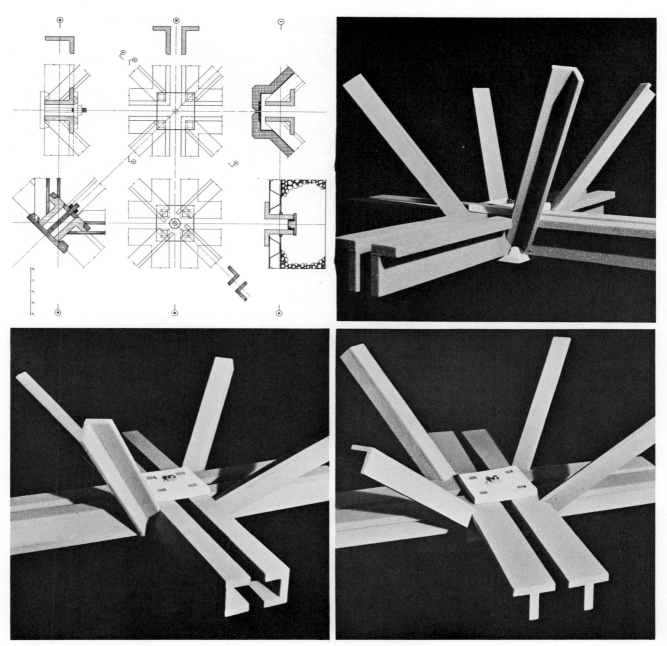

Plate 23
1. Detail of node utilizing angle components. 2. Node using angle components. 3. Node using channel components. 4. Node using tee components.

Plate 24
UNISTRUT space frame system. A two-way space grid with all framing
members of the same length and identical cross section. It has
identical connectors so designed as to require one bolt at each end of
each member. The units are manufactured on a special jig resulting
in a small and precise tolerance. It is self-aligning and self-leveling.

30

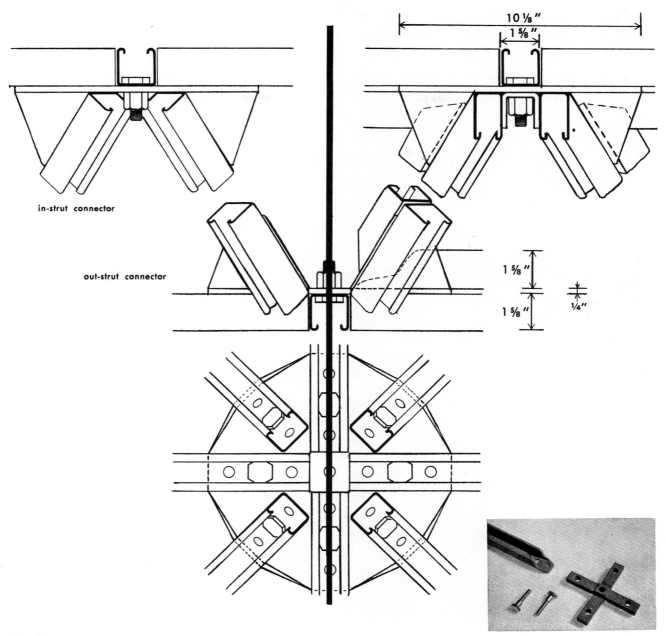

in-strut connector

out-strut connector

10 ⅛ "

1 ⅝ "

1 ⅝ "

1 ⅝ "

¼"

Plate 25
Details of the UNISTRUT connector. The left-hand side of the drawing
shows a standard joint. A series of reinforcing parts both for the
strut and the connector (shown), can be added to the basic space frame
resulting in a reinforced joint, right-hand side of drawing.

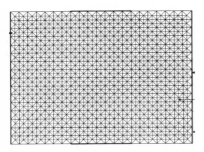

Plate 26
The generating cell of the UNISTRUT space frame system. A cell
whose members form the edges of alternating erect and inverted
pentahedrons (square pyramids), whose bases create a series of
tetrahedrons (triangular pyramids) that interlock with the pentahedrons.
The unit cell is formed by two octahedrons (inverted pentahedrons
and two tetrahedrons).

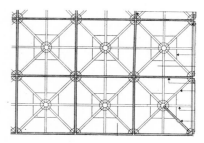

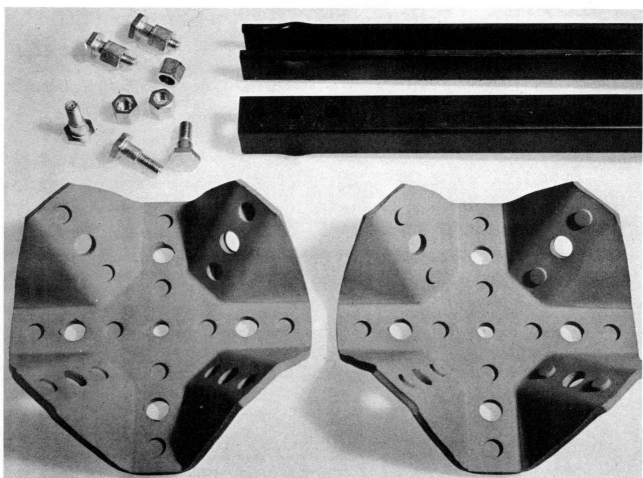

Plate 27
The five UNISTRUT space frame parts: out-strut connector, instrut connector, strut, bolt and nut.

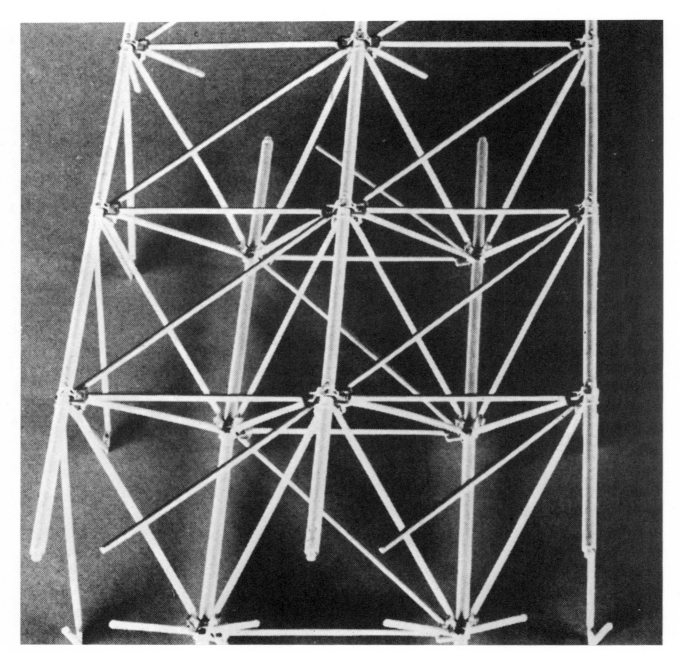

Plate 28
Project by Konrad Wachsmann—a space structure system for large hangars. The tetrahedral system of the space frame. Up to 20 members can be joined in a single node in any combination with a constant modular distance of ten feet between nodes. The structure is basically another version of a two-way space grid, stiffened by additional members subdividing the top and bottom square grid into two triangles.

Plate 29
The standard joint with an upper clip for attaching panels, etc. This
attempt at prefabrication at that time by Wachsmann has been of
great importance. Though this connector is very complicated, it paved the
way for further improvements that led eventually to the ingenious
MERO and TRIODETIC systems.

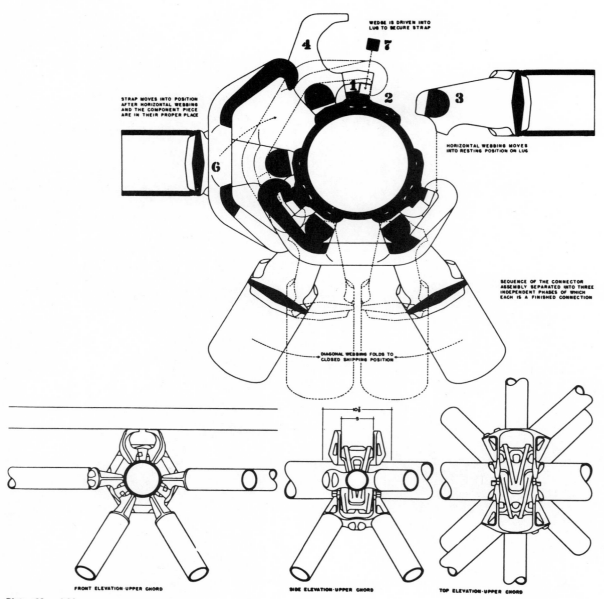

WEDGE IS DRIVEN INTO
LUG TO SECURE STRAP

4

7

1

2

3

STRAP MOVES INTO POSITION
AFTER HORIZONTAL WEBBING
AND THE COMPONENT PIECE
ARE IN THEIR PROPER PLACE

HORIZONTAL WEBBING MOVES
INTO RESTING POSITION ON LUG

6

SEQUENCE OF THE CONNECTOR
ASSEMBLY SEPARATED INTO THREE
INDEPENDENT PHASES OF WHICH
EACH IS A FINISHED CONNECTION

DIAGONAL WEBBING FOLDS TO
CLOSED SHIPPING POSITION

FRONT ELEVATION·UPPER CHORD

SIDE ELEVATION·UPPER CHORD

TOP ELEVATION·UPPER CHORD

Plates 30 and 31
Sections through the standard connection showing the principle,
the sequence of assembly, and the way in which the diagonal webbing
folds. Also shown are details of the combination of members at
upper and lower chords.

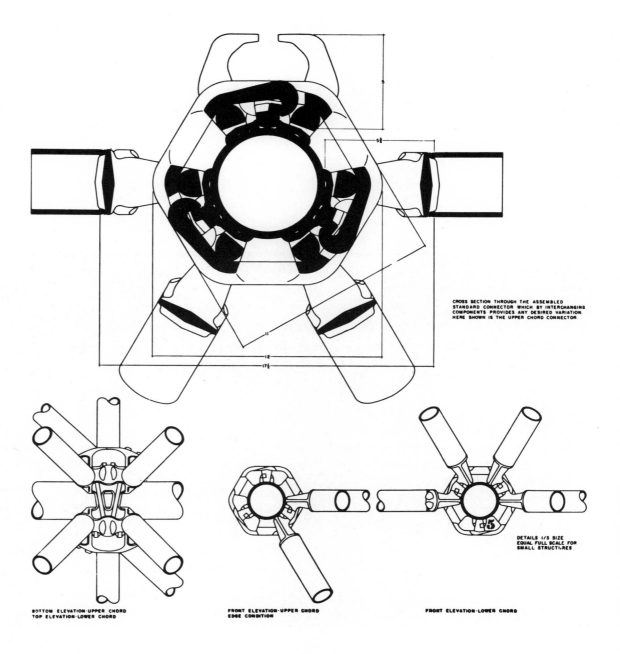

CROSS SECTION THROUGH THE ASSEMBLED
STANDARD CONNECTOR WHICH BY INTERCHANGING
COMPONENTS PROVIDES ANY DESIRED VARIATION.
HERE SHOWN IS THE UPPER CHORD CONNECTOR.

BOTTOM ELEVATION·UPPER CHORD
TOP ELEVATION·LOWER CHORD

FRONT ELEVATION·UPPER CHORD
EDGE CONDITION

FRONT ELEVATION·LOWER CHORD

DETAILS 1/3 SIZE
EQUAL FULL SCALE FOR
SMALL STRUCTURES

Plate 31

37

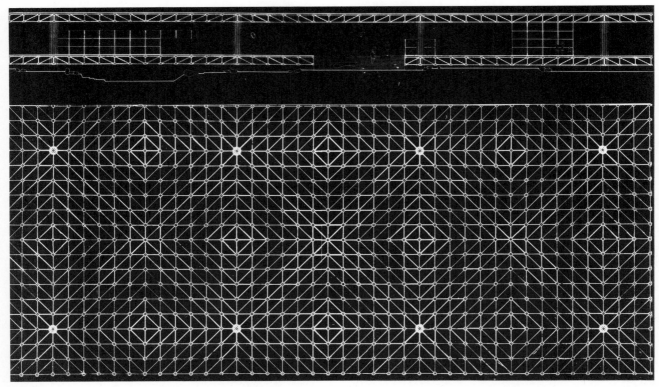

Plate 32
Team project at L'Ecole Polytechnique de l'Université de Lausanne under Konrad Wachsmann, 1959. The study of a space frame for a pavilion. A vertical and horizontal view of construction. The variation between thick and thin lines in the plan indicates the use of 1, 2, or 3 construction rods according to static demands. The space structure is made up of vertical intersecting trusses with the top and bottom a square grid subdivided into triangles that create the tetrahedrons.

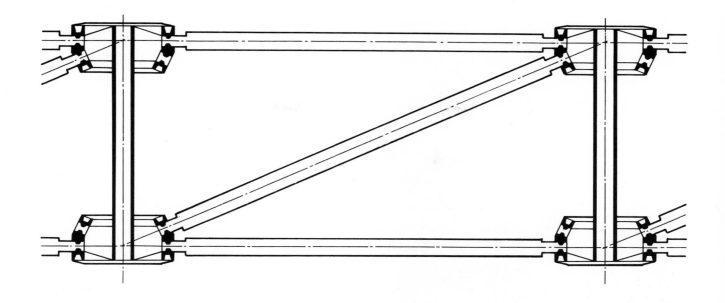

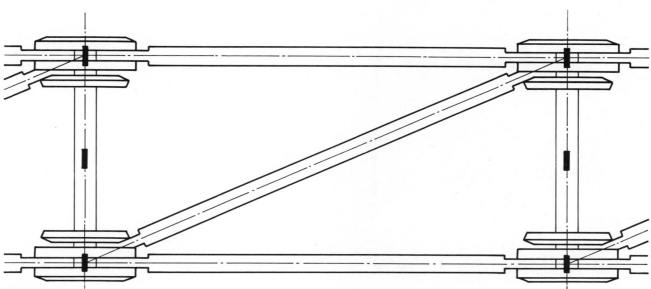

Plate 33
Section and elevation of the basic cell and connection that form
the horizontal space frame.

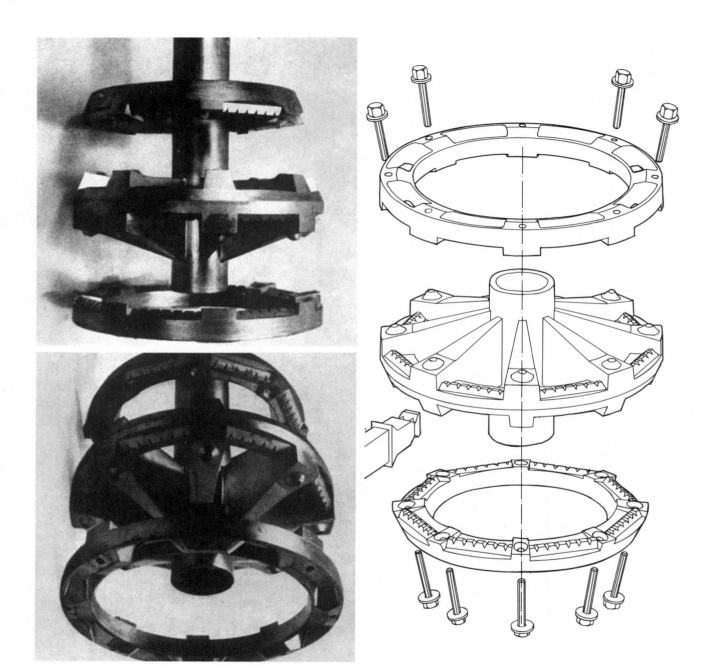

Plate 34
1. and 2. The knot connector opened to expose the 3 basic elements of the connector, a top ring, a hub connected to the vertical tube, and a bottom ring. 3. Isometric of the knot showing the bolt connection of the top and bottom rings to the central hub.

Plate 35
1. Standard knot of structure. 2. and 4. Representation of the combination
of utilization possibilities of 1 to 3 forcing or draw rods according
to static demands. 3. End view of construction rods.

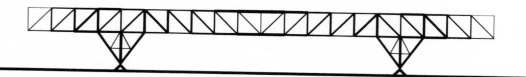

Plate 36
Team project by Phil Brown, Henry Ferrera, Armando Gonzales, Jon
Jerde, Robert Kraft, Richard Smith at the University of Southern
California under Konrad Wachsmann, 1965. A long span structure with
minimum support having maximum usable space within and below the
structure for an undefined function. A space frame with a span of
720 ft and cantilevers of 240 ft, module 60 ft.

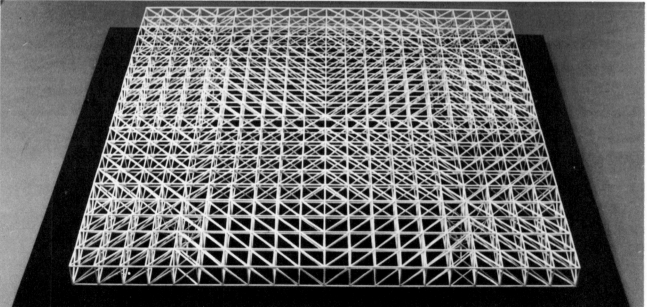

Plate 37
1. Views of the over-all structure as seen from ground level. 2. Aerial view of space structure. The tetrahedral subdivision of the cube provides the basis for the development of this structure. It provides a reasonable balance between structural efficiency and large spaces with an orderly subdivision of rectangular spaces. This is possible because the diagonal is in a right-angled vertical plane.

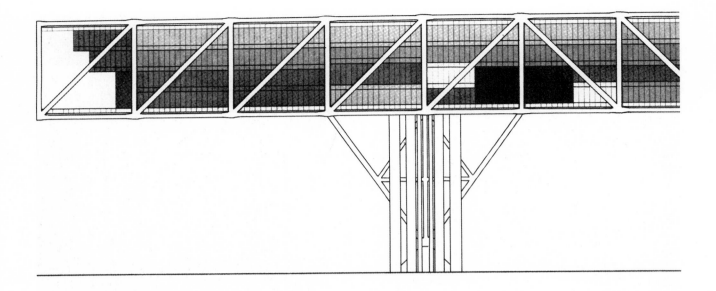

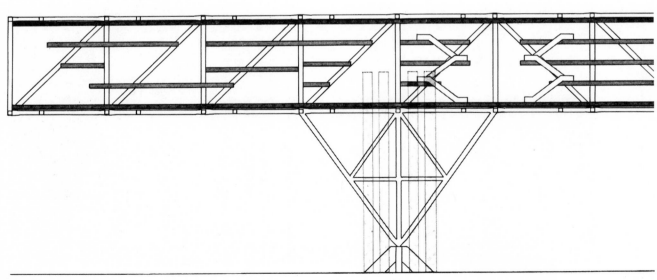

Plate 38
Partial elevation and section of the space frame illustrating the usable
space within the structure.

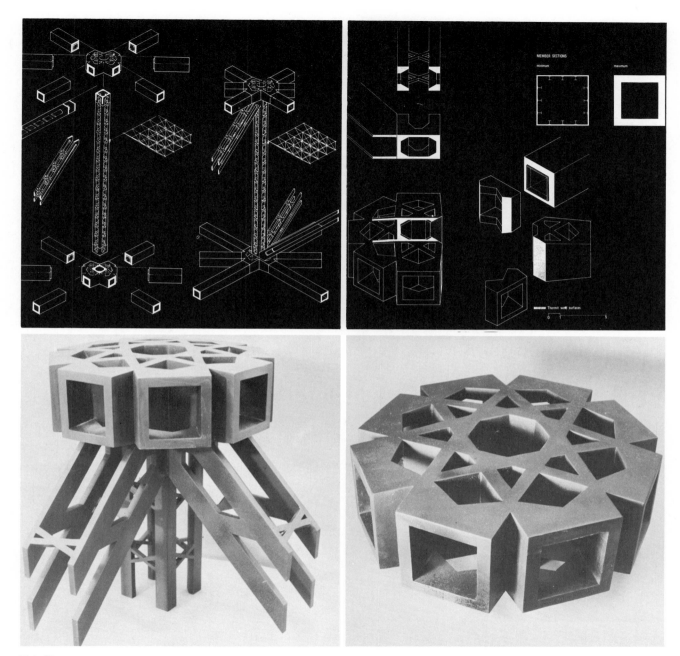

Plate 39
1. Components of the major structure. 2. Joint of the major structure
showing thermit-welded surfaces. 3.—4. Joint of the major structure.

45

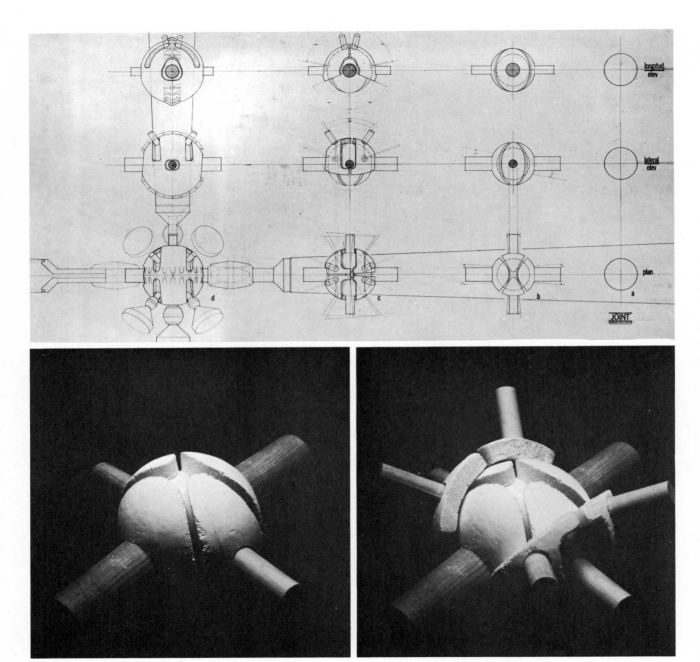

Plate 40

Project by Richard Smith at the University of Southern California under Konrad Wachsmann, 1965. The joint from a long span prefabricated concrete structure. A joint in which all members know only one point in space in compression or tension. The struts are arranged around a sphere in the center and the layers are sealed by caps that resist tension. 1. Details of the joint. 2.—3. Views of joint illustrating the central sphere.

46

Plate 41
View of the joint illustrating how the various spherical plates are
arranged around the central ball and are finally sealed to the ball by
caps that allow the passage and movement of the strut connectors
coming into the node at various angles.

Plate 42
Team project at the University of Tokyo under Konrad Wachsmann, 1955.
Study of a building system for a school pavilion. View of the building
showing the open floor and roof construction.

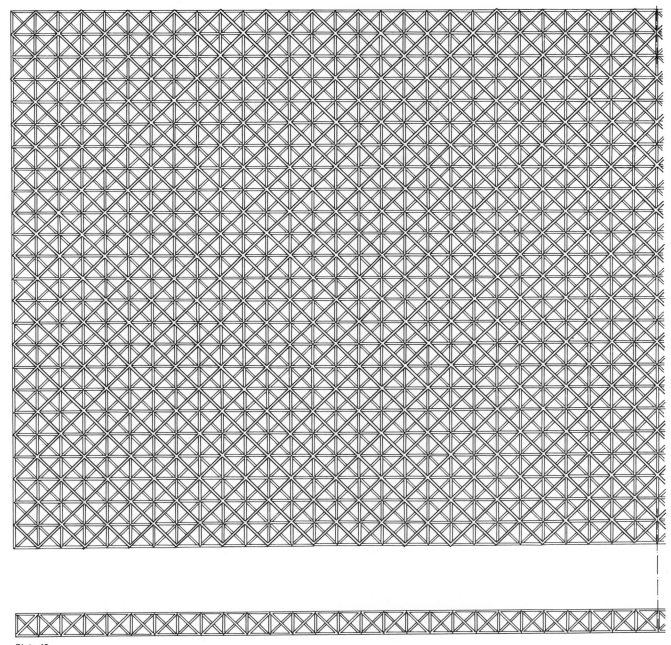

Plate 43
Plan and elevation of one-half of the horizontal space frame, a
two-way space grid turned at 45° to the edge.

Plate 44
The horizontal space frame is of lightweight aluminum construction based
on a standard connection.

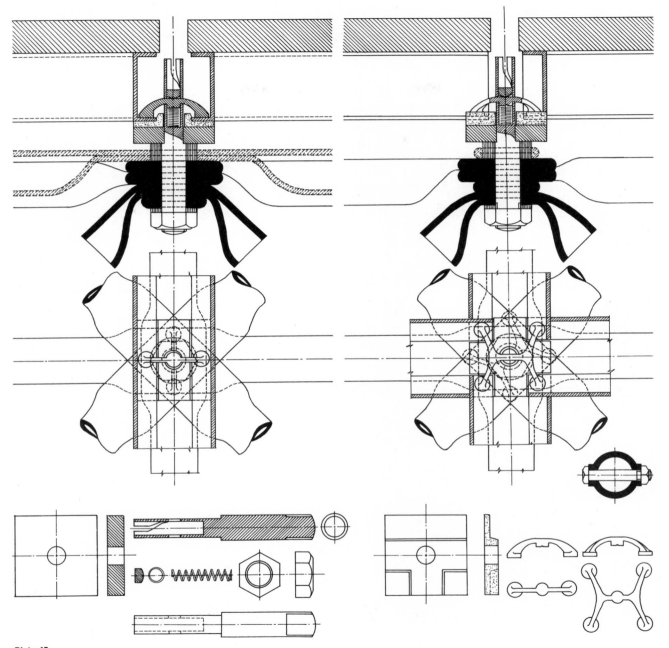

Plate 45
A section and view of the connection and securing of the floor tiles. The system is of flattened aluminum tubes held together by means of a vertical pin. Below are the metal parts that hold a floor tile to the construction.

51

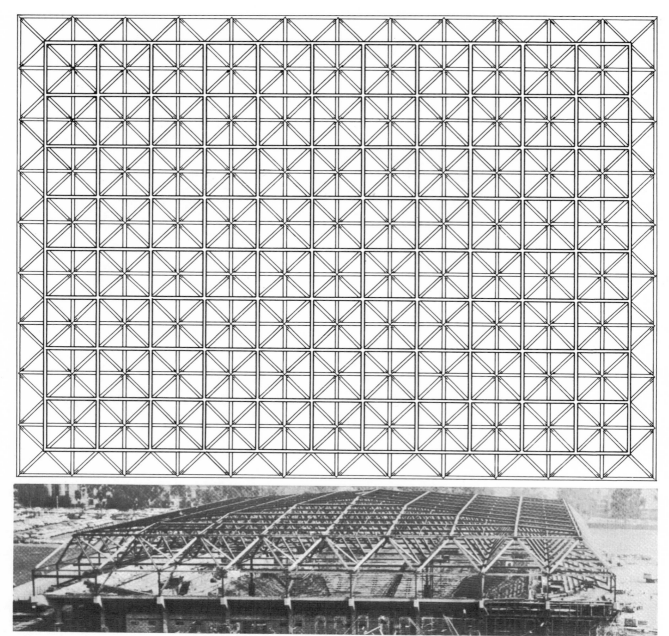

Plate 46
Project by Welton Beckett and Associates. The space frame provides a
300 × 400 ft clear span area for an auditorium sports pavilion at the
University of California at Los Angeles. Basically the space frame
is a series of steel H-sections interlaced to form 108 interconnected
pyramids in plan. All bays are 33'—4" sq and the space frame is
9 bays × 12 bays. The space frame is 30 ft deep in the center and 17
ft deep along the perimeter.

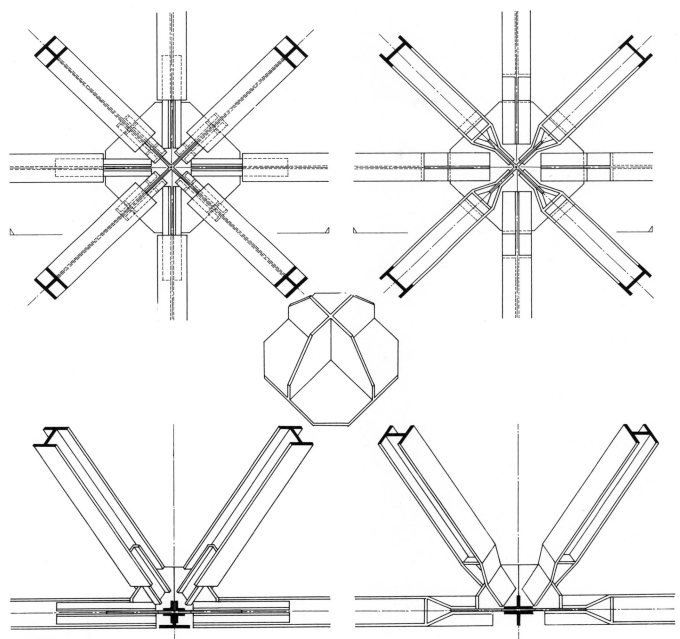

Plate 47
Details of the space frame. The framing consists of 10 WF to 14 WF members; to avoid conjestion at the joints, smaller sized hubs were used for attachment to a three-dimensional gusset plate with high tensile bolts. On the left are the details used throughout the structure; the details on the right are for the peripheral exposed bays.

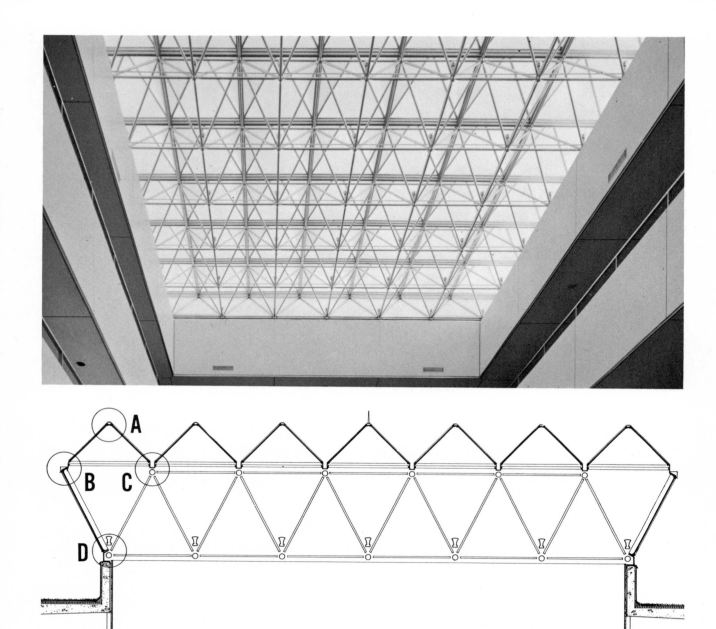

Plate 48
Project by Minoro Yamasaki. An aluminum two-way space grid forming
the skylight for the Regional Sales Office Building, Reynolds Metals Co.,
Southfield, 1959. The space grid is fabricated of aluminum tubes and
connecting spheres. 1. Photo of the space grid. 2. Section through
the structure.

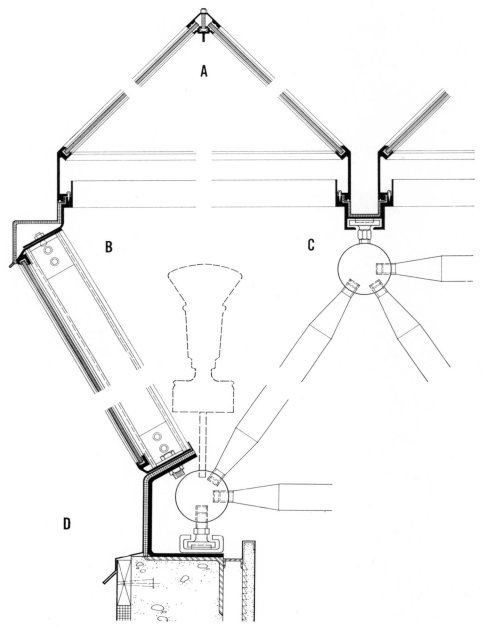

Plate 49
The structural details of the two-way space grid. The connectors
are 3 ½'' tapped aluminum spheres, the struts are 1 ¾" in diameter.
The entire grid is on a 5' × 5' module.

Study of a Structural Bay

School of Design, North Carolina State College

Developed under Horacio Caminos with students of the fifth-year class, 1961.

Goal

To incorporate in the true structure, space for ducts and pipes using the total height of the space between floor and ceiling.

Assumptions and limitations of the problem (based upon experience) are
a. Bay—48' × 48'
b. Material-reinforced concrete
c. Two-way system
d. Maximum use of precast elements, minimum of concrete poured in place
e. Pre- or post-stress methods—optional
f. Module 6' and 12'
g. Perforations in the structure to allow the passage of ducts, pipes, conduits

HORIZONTAL in two directions—a minimum of 0.25 sq ft per linear foot, including two perforations of a minimum of 5 sq ft each.

VERTICAL a minimum of 2 perforations 1 sq ft each.
h. 12-ft cantilever in one or two sides to study column connections.
Within the preceding limitations, two types of solutions are schematically presented.
a. Two-way space trusses 6' × 6' grid
b. Two-way space trusses 12' × 12' grid
It should be made clear that the elements and molds were adapted to the small scale of the molds ½" = 1'. Therefore they do not attempt to reproduce the problems of a full-scale construction. Nevertheless the exercise is still valid because it is an experience in the handling and forming of concrete, although in a different scale, and the form is a result of requirements, assumptions, materials, and method of construction.

Some general recommendations were formulated that are valid for full-scale construction:
a. The major problems are at the column connections.
b. Elements that can be laid down on a horizontal plane are recommended.
c. The elements generally are a precast slab forming the top chord and a precast pyramid forming the diagonals and bottom chord.

Plate 50
A two-way concrete space frame as a floor system with the columns
positioned. The basic unit is a precast concrete tetrahedron (triangular
pyramid) which is post-tensioned in two directions.

Plate 51
1. View of space frame with precast floor slabs removed, showing
post-tensioning steel in two directions and the arrangement of the
precast tetrahedron units at the column supports. 2. View looking up at
the assembled two-way space frame, showing the bottom grid and
edge condition.

Plate 52
The basic unit, a precast concrete tetrahedron unit, which is post-
tensioned in two directions.

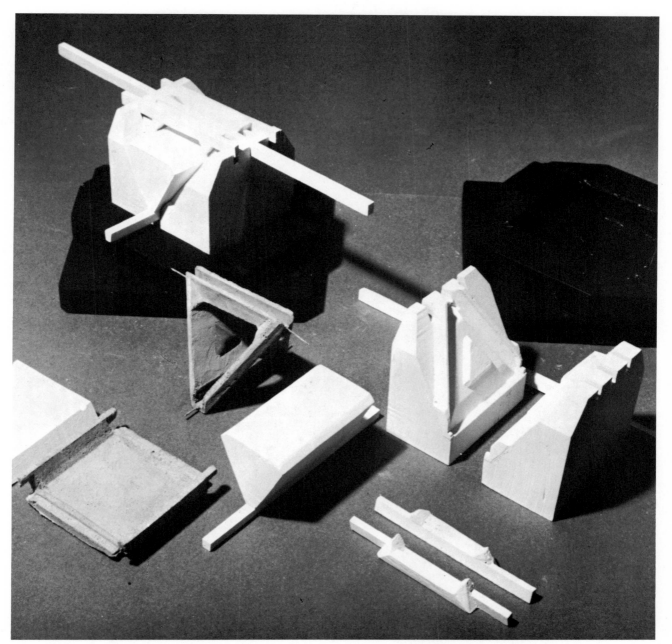

Plate 53
The formwork for the precast tetrahedron unit and the precast floor
slab, shown assembled and disassembled, revealing the components
of the formwork, and the precast unit.

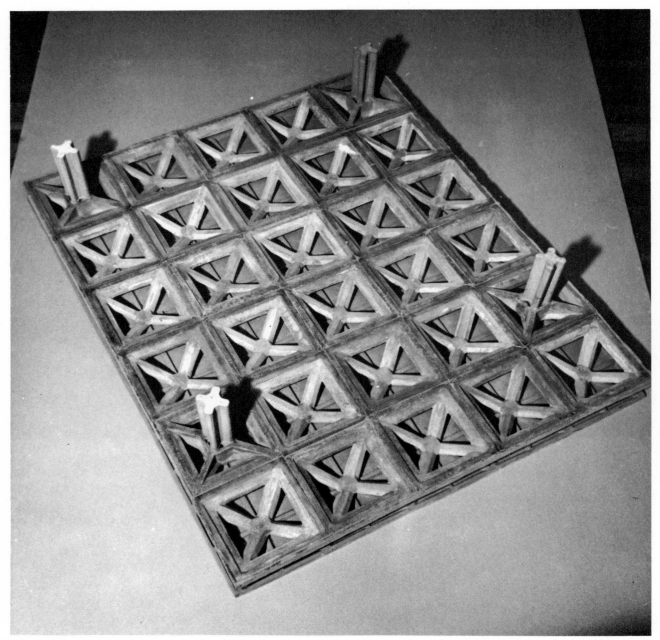

Plate 54
A two-way concrete space frame as a floor system with the columns
positioned. The basic unit is a precast pentahedron (square pyramid)
which is post-tensioned in two directions.

Plate 55
1. Concrete space frame showing column units and regular pentahedron units. 2. Formwork and underside of precast pentahedron unit.

Plate 56

1. A two-way concrete space frame of pentahedron units (square pyramids). The precast pyramids are set in place, reinforcing added, bottom grid poured, floor slabs set, and top grid poured. The edge units are poured in place. When cured, the system is post-tensioned.

2. Formwork for precast pyramid and slab. 3. The combination of pyramids and slabs with the resulting tetrahedron units. The reinforcing top and bottom is cast in place to form the top and bottom grids.

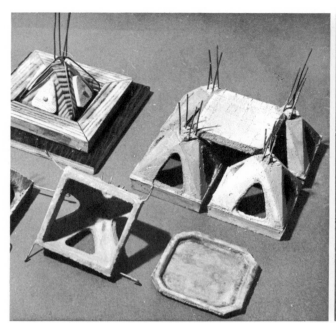

Plate 57
1. Formwork and component of a two-way precast concrete space frame. 2. Component of a two-way concrete space frame in which alternate pentahedrons (square pyramids) are removed. 3. Lineal concrete trusses, which when combined form long pyramidal trusses with the bottom grid formed by short precast units and top grid formed by precast slab units. This is post-tensioned in the direction perpendicular to the lineal trusses to form a two-way space frame system.

65

Study of a Structural Bay
Massachusetts Institute of Technology

Under Horacio Caminos with fourth-year students in
the School of Architecture and Planning, 1964.

The problem is to study a structural bay and its method
of construction under the following assumptions:

a. The bay will be repeated at least 40 times in a
building three or four stories high. The major functional
requirement of the building will be flexibility of space
and use. Flexibility means that not only should the
partitions be movable, but provisions should be made to
supply any of the installed physical services to all
areas of the building (heating, cooling, mechanical
ventilation, electricity, cold and hot water, etc.). In
addition to this, the design should be so conceived that
the space could be divided into both large and small
areas.

b. Material: Reinforced concrete. Type of structure: two-
way system. Technique of construction: use of precast
elements; pre- or post-stressing, optional. Cast-in-place
concrete should be minimized.

c. Dimensions: Square bay 48′ × 48′ (center to center of
columns). Structural module: 6′ × 6′. Two sides of
the bay should have a 12′ or a 9′ cantilever. Height of
the structural slab: 5′. Height of column: 10′. The
structure should have perforations in two directions to
permit the passage of horizontal ducts and pipes of 4
square feet in section. Columns should provide space
for vertical pipes 8″ in diameter (drainage, water
supply, etc.).

d. Within the preceding limitations, two types of solutions
are presented:

Type a.—Two-way space trusses on a 12′ × 12′ grid.
Type b.—Two-way space trusses on a 6′ × 6′ grid.

Plate 58
A two-way concrete space frame on a 12′ × 12′ structural grid. Shown
is part of a bay with two column supports, formwork for the
precast pentahedron (square pyramid) unit, and a typical unit of the
space frame.

Plate 59
A two-way concrete space frame on a 6' × 6' structural grid. Shown is part of a bay with two column supports, the formwork for the precast pentahedron (square pyramid) unit, the column and the slab, with a typical pyramid and floor slab of the space frame.

Plate 60
View looking up at the two-way concrete space grid showing the end
elevation, bottom grid formed by the pyramids and the column supports.

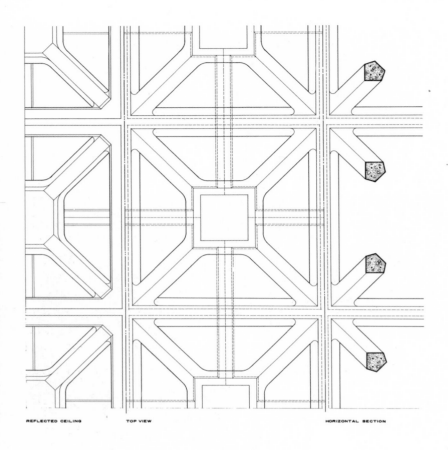

REFLECTED CEILING   TOP VIEW   HORIZONTAL SECTION

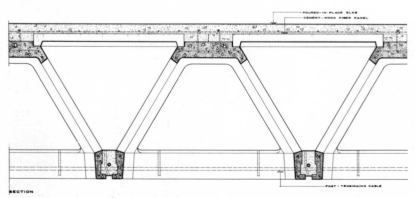

POURED-IN-PLACE SLAB
CEMENT-WOOD FIBER PANEL

SECTION   POST-TENSIONING CABLE

Plate 61
Project by Robert P. Burns under Eduardo Catalano at the Massachusetts
Institute of Technology, 1962. Typical precast pentahedron (square
pyramid) unit from a two-way concrete space frame for a precast
floor system.

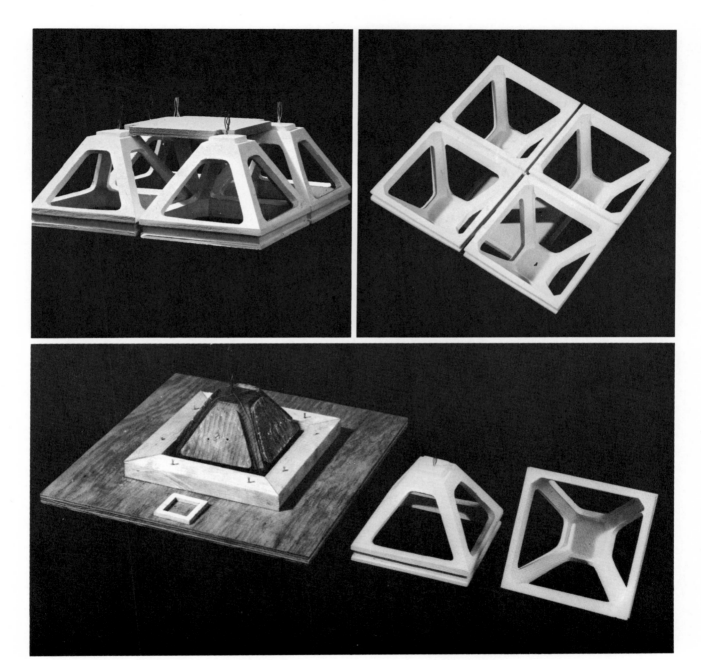

Plate 62
1. The combination of precast pyramid units and slabs with the resulting tetrahedron units. The slabs form the top grid of the space frame.
2. View looking up into the precast pyramids which form the bottom grid of the space frame. 3. The formwork for and views of the precast concrete pyramid unit.

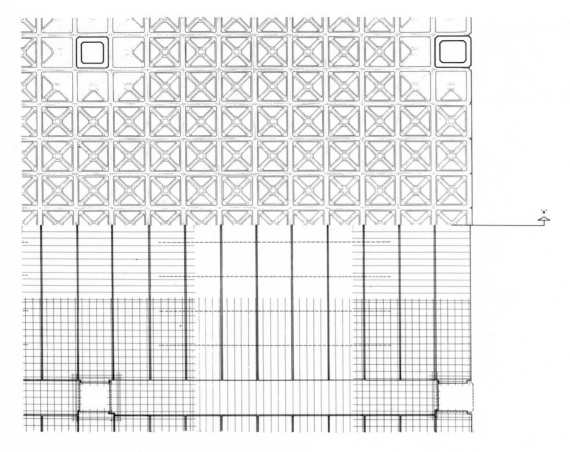

REFLECTED CEILING PLAN, COMPONENT PLACEMENT, PRINCIPAL REINFORCEMENT

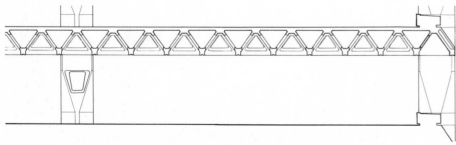

SECTION 'A'

Plate 63
Project by Phillip A. Kupritz under Eduardo Catalano at the Massachusetts
Institute of Technology, 1962. A precast two-way space frame
constructed of linear beam components. A 50′ × 50′ bay with a
5′ × 5′ structural grid.

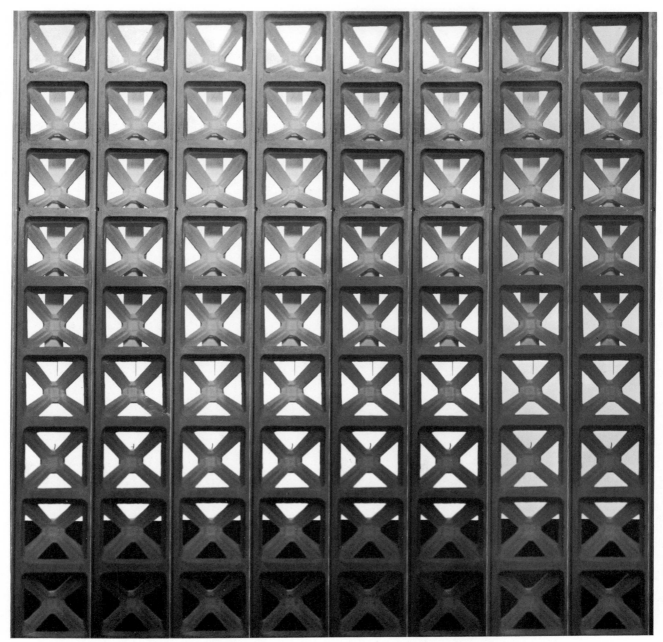

Plate 64
Reflected ceiling plan of the two-way concrete space frame.

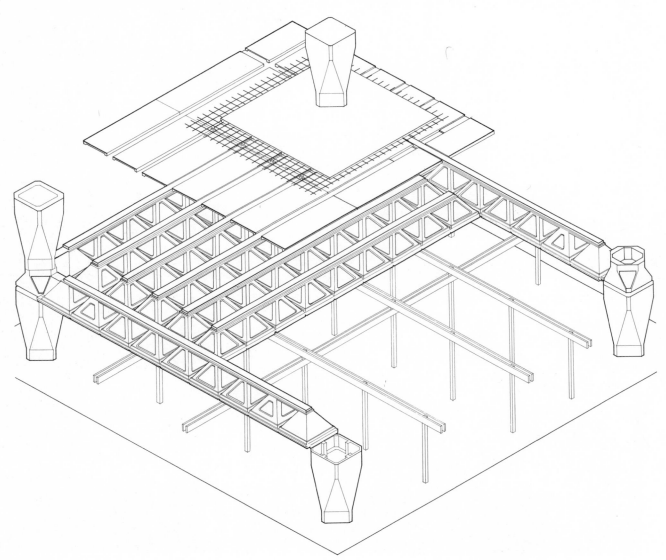

Plate 65
Isometric view of the construction sequence for the two-way concrete space frame. The steps are A. Anchor column to foundation. B. Erect shoring supporting beam ends. C. Place trussed frame units. (Place next column and column steel). D. Position post-tension cables.

E. Grout lower ribs and place cone around columns. F. Place top slabs. G. Bend steel to be on slab panels. (Place negative reinforcement). H. Pour 3" top slab. I. Post-tension cables after slab is properly cured. J. Repeat procedure.

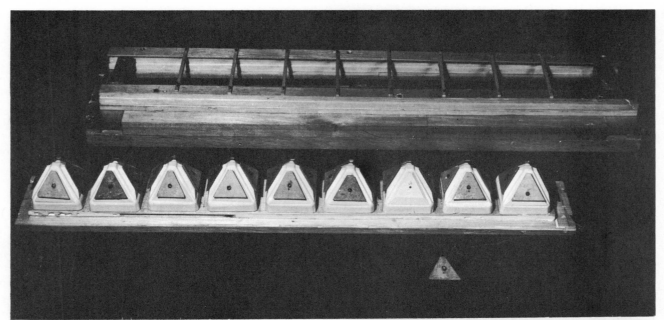

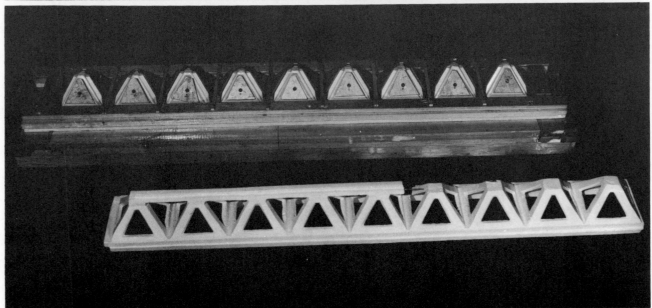

Plate 66
Formwork and typical precast linear beam component showing the
two stages of fabrication. 1. Linear beams are poured with pyramidal
units. 2. The tops of the individual pyramids are tied together by a beam.

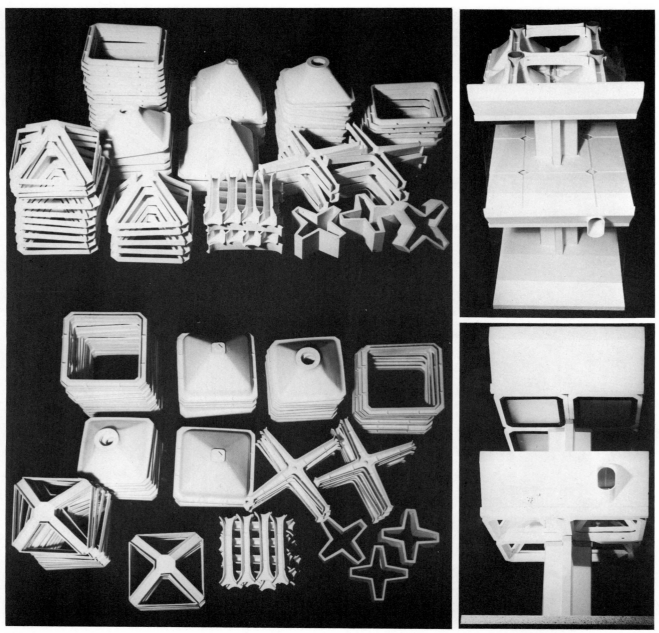

Plate 67
Project by Edward Popko at the University of Detroit, 1967. A study
of a precast concrete building system whose elements form a
two-way space grid structure. 1. Precast elements for three floor and
roof systems. 2.—3. Models showing two of the space frame systems;
one a skeletal system, the stressed-skin system.

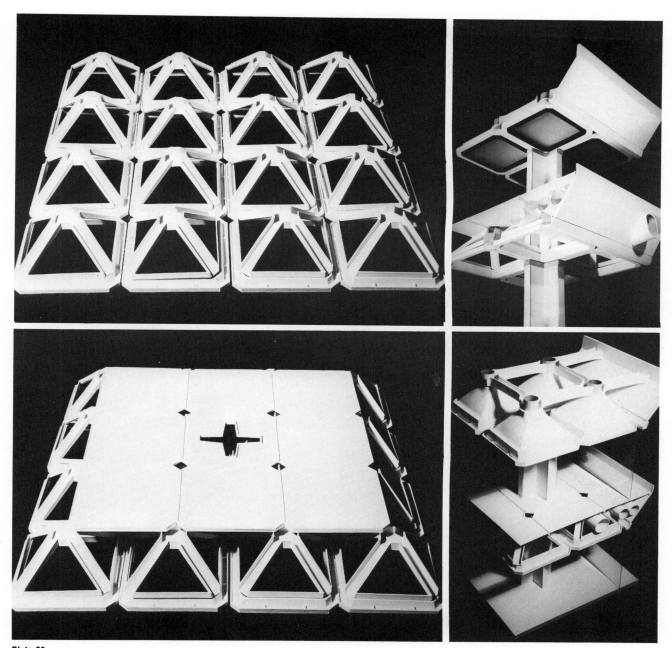

Plate 68

1.–2. Models showing mechanical system running through the space frame, the column support, and openings at the apex of the stressed-skin pyramids to allow the penetration of natural light. 3. A precast system of formwork which allows identical elements to be produced. The horizontal and inclined troughs, which are formed by the form-adapter base and the square-based pyramid form, allow a variation in steel layout as required by the stresses in different structural bays. 4. The apexes of the square-based pyramid formwork are interconnected by slabs which allow the penetration of steel that is tied into the floor slab. This system addresses itself to the variations in stresses in a concrete space frame.

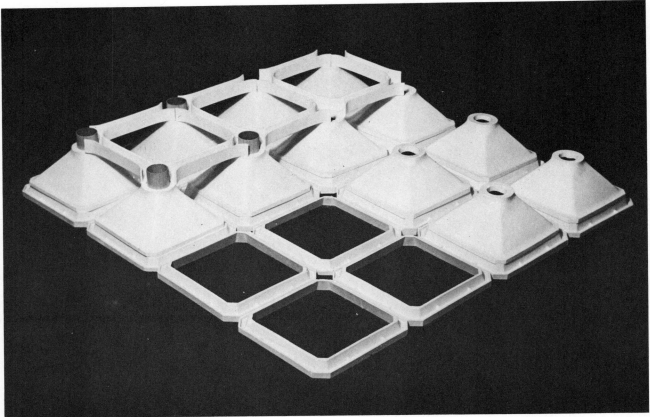

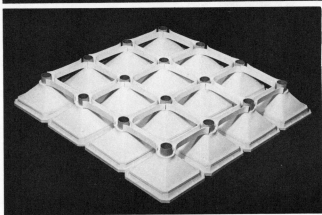

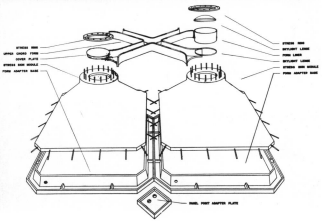

Plate 69
1. A precast concrete space frame whose component elements are a form-adapter base, a stressed skin module, and an upper chord form.
2. Assembled units of this structural system. 3. Axonometric of the stressed-skin space frame showing all the elements in this system.

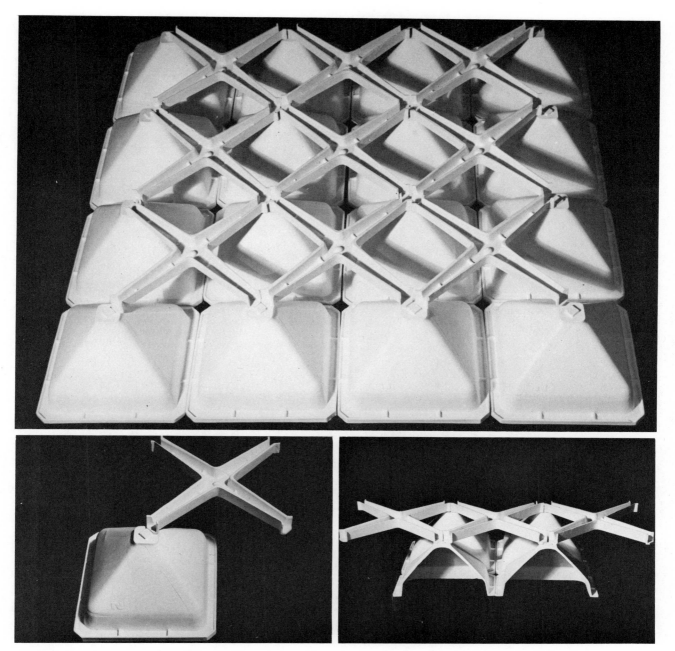

Plate 70
1. A precast concrete space frame whose component elements are
2. A stressed-skin square-based pyramid and an upper chord form.
3. Assembly showing cut-away stressed-skin units and the troughs
for the placing of the reinforcing steel.

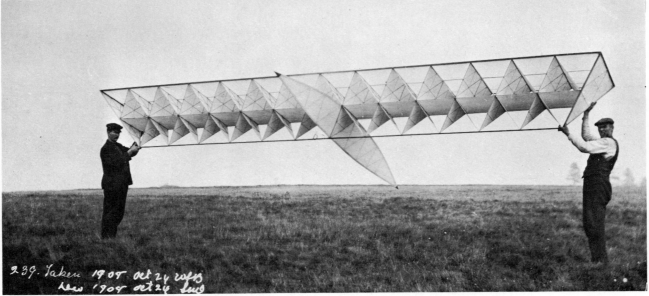

Plate 71
Projects by Alexander Graham Bell. Bell concerned himself with space structures based on the tetrahedron. He developed space frames having combinations of axially loaded members by themselves and in combination with stressed-skin systems. 1. A three-way space frame constructed of metal rods and connectors. 2. A model constructed in 1908 during the period when Dr. Bell and his colleagues in the Aerial Experiment Association were building successful powered biplanes. The model reflects an experimental wedding of kite and airplane design. (Photographs courtesy of the National Geographic Society, Washington, D.C.)

Plate 72
Bell recognized the extraordinary strength of these structural systems. He mass-produced prefabricated standardized tetrahedral units of rods, tubes, and stressed skin. He illustrated how to make simpler, lighter, and stronger structures made possible by the machine and industrialization. 1. The tetrahedral observation tower, built from prefabricated tetrahedrons, lies on the ground ready to be raised, 1907. 2. Tetrahedral cells to be used in the construction of Dr. Bell's observation tower at Beinn Bhreagh.

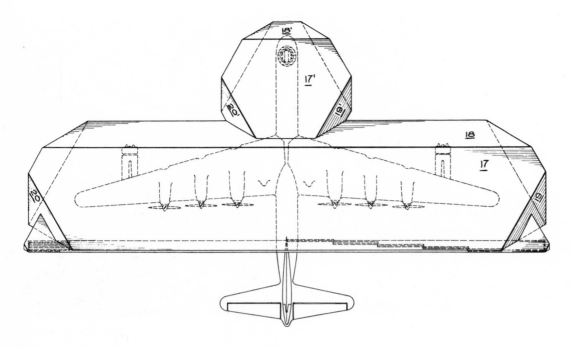

FIG. 1

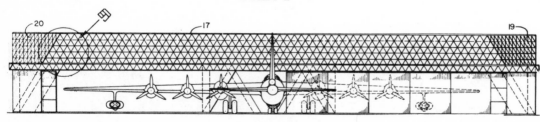

FIG. 2

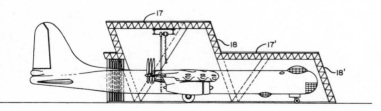

FIG. 3

Plate 73
Project by Richard Buckminster Fuller. A roof, wall and/or floor
framework consisting of a truss in which the main structural elements,
struts or triangular sheet members, form equilateral triangles interconnected in a pattern consisting of octahedrons and tetrahedrons, with
the major axes of all octahedrons parallel throughout the octetruss

framework. Fig. 1. A plan view of a servicing dock for a B-36 bomber;
the roof and walls of the dock are constructed with the octetruss.
Fig. 2. Front elevation of the dock. Fig. 3. Vertical section through
the center of the dock.

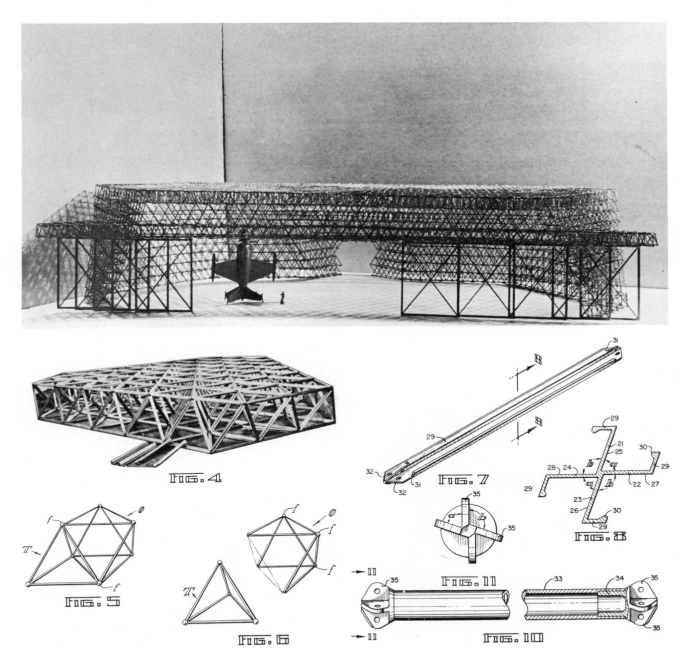

Plate 74

1. Model of the dock. Fig. 4. A perspective view of a representative truss section of the roof and wall framework. Fig. 5. One of the octahedrons and conjoined tetrahedrons of the truss. Fig. 6. Separate views of the octahedra and tetrahedra units. Fig. 7. A perspective view of one of the struts in Fig. 4. Fig. 8. A cross-section of the strut in Fig. 7. Fig. 10. A side view of a modified strut. Fig. 11. An end view of the strut in Fig. 10.

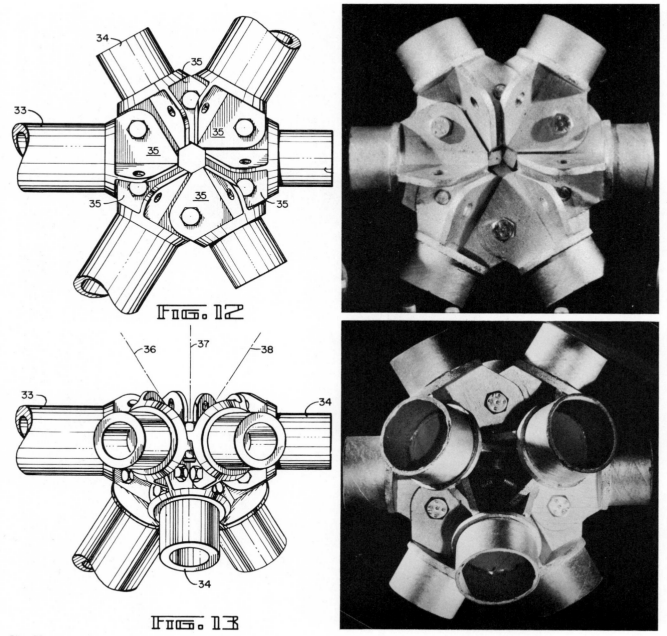

FIG. 12

FIG. 13

Plate 75
Fig. 12. A plan view of a connection. Fig. 13. A side elevation of the same connection. 1. A model in plan of connection. 2. A model in side elevation of same connection.

Plate 76
1. Models of strut, end connector, and partially completed nodes.
2.—3. Models showing how a strut intersects and becomes part of the node.

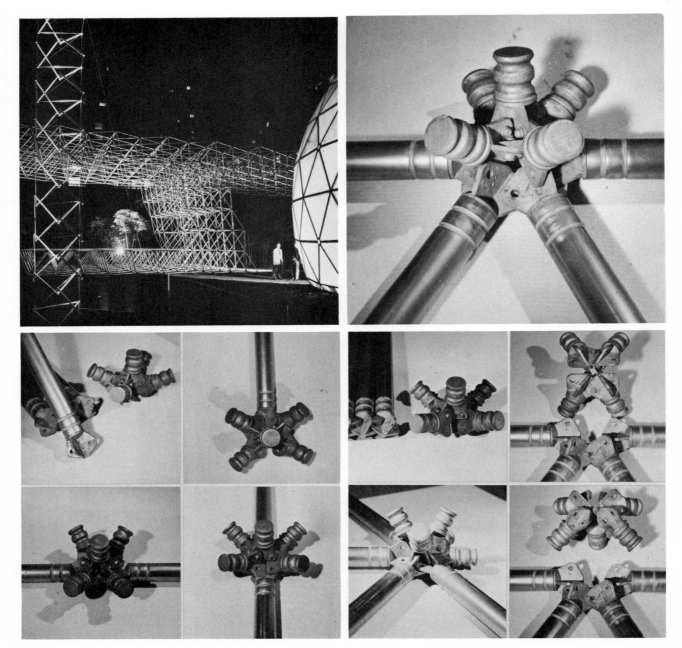

Plate 77
1. Octetruss structure by Richard Buckminster Fuller, 100' long, 35' wide, cantilevered 60' one way, 40' the other, fabricated from 2" tubes. Fuller Exhibition, Museum of Modern Art, New York, 1959.
2.—4. Views of the component elements for the node in this octetruss.

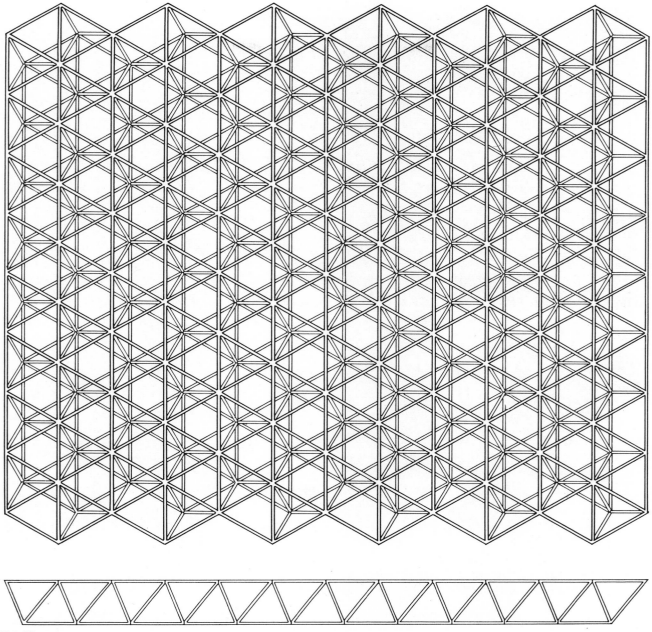

Plate 78
Partial plan and elevation of the octetruss, a three-way double-layer
space frame constructed of aluminum tubes of all the same length.

Plate 79
The TRIODETIC system by S. Fentiman and Sons, Ltd., of Ottawa, Canada, is based on a simple connection that can be made without any welds, bolts, or rivets. Members to be joined are prepared in a pressing operation that forms the metal to fit the slots in the connector hubs. Member lengths and end angles are controlled automatically in a factory operation giving great precision in the end structural assembly without any need for forms or jigs. In erection the members are inserted into the extruded hubs under slight pressure. 1. Three-way space frame assembly. 2. The three-way connector used in assembly. 3. Alternate method of accomplishing the same joint. This is the most successful connector developed so far for metal space frame construction.

Plate 80
Any member or members may be joined at a single point in space, radiating at almost any angle, with a single connector. 1. The various extruded aluminum hubs used in the different geometric layouts. 2. A hub with 6 struts. 3. Connection with washers bolted on both ends of the extrusion to keep struts from unlocking. 4. Extrusion welded to larger structural section.

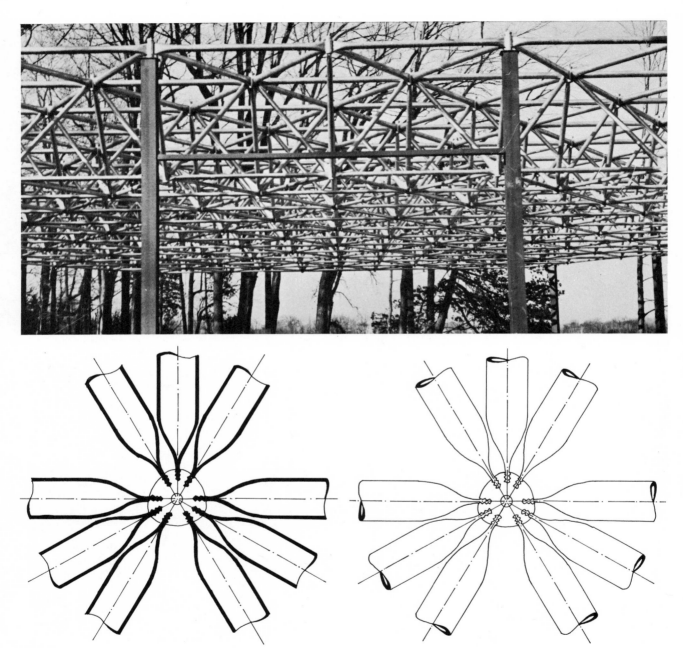

Plate 81

1. A three-way double-layer space grid that is formed with this system. Auditorium Building, Ontario. Hexagonal plan, 36' to a side, 6' module, 4"—4 ¼' depth. 2. Plan of a three-way TRIODETIC connector that may be employed in this grid. 3. Section through the connection showing how the extruded aluminum or steel hub may receive the struts, which are stamped and slotted to fit into the slotted connector. The strut tapers with no material removed or added.

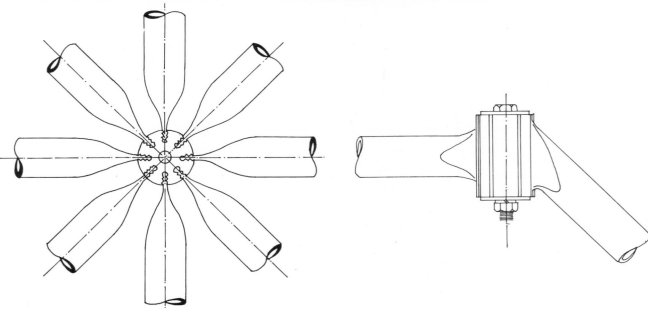

Plate 82
1. Two-way double-layer space grids, 118′ × 118′ and 118′ ×
86′–0″, module 8′, depth of grid 4′–0″ for a university gymnasium in
Canada. 2. Plan of a two-way TRIODETIC connector, which may be
employed in this grid. 3. Side elevation showing how the horizontal
and inclined struts meet the connector.

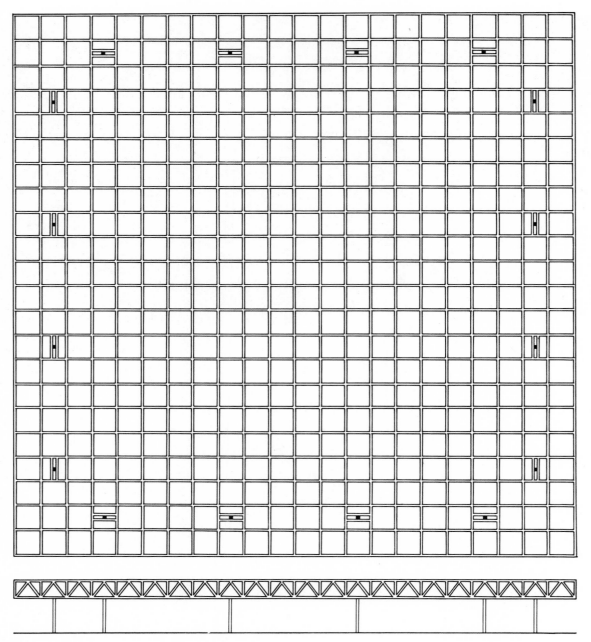

Plate 83
Project by Skidmore, Owings and Merrill. A two-way space frame of
vertical intersecting trusses for the Air Force Academy dining hall
roof. This space frame has 46 steel trusses intersecting at right angles
on a 14' module. It is 308' square and rests on 16 steel columns.
The space frame has an interior span of 252' $\times$ 252' with a 22'
cantilever on all four sides. Ceiling height is 24'.

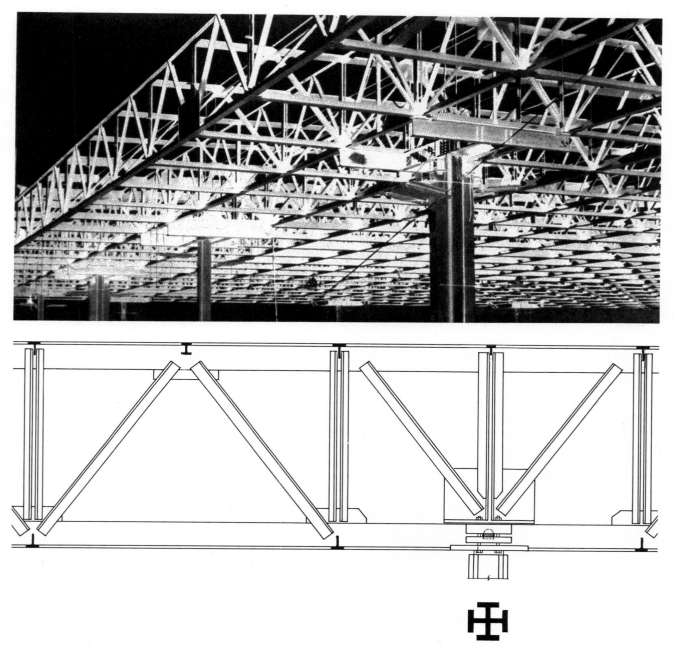

Plate 84
1. Space frame shown in place. The structure was elevated into position using the columns as jacks. 2. Detail of the welded intersecting trusses showing the truss fabrication, column connection and column section.

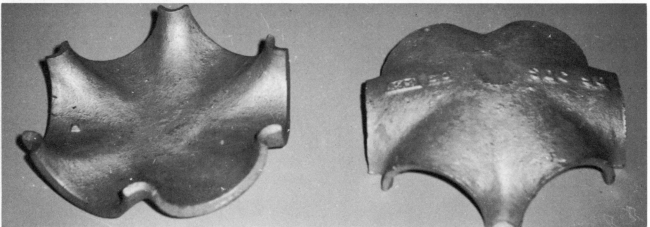

Plate 85
The Tridirectionnelle S.D.C. system for connecting three-way double-
layer lattice space grids or three-way single-layer grids, developed
by M. S. du Chateau, France. 1. A lattice space grid of intersecting
vertical trusses forming a three-way double-layer network. The geometry
of the S.D.C. system. 2. The S.D.C. connectors, up to 13 struts intersect
at the node. Photo shows views of the cast joint.

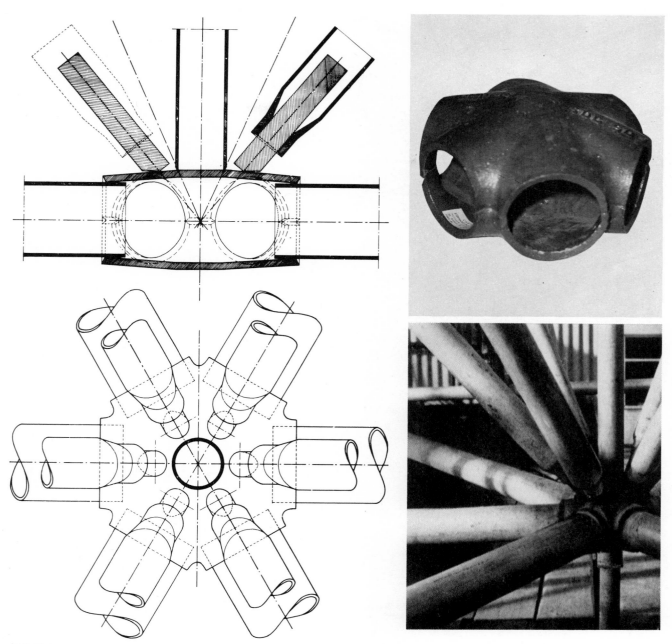

Plate 86
1. Details of the S.D.C. node with 13 elements intersecting at the node. 2. View of the S.D.C. connector. 3. View of the node showing the 13 intersecting struts.

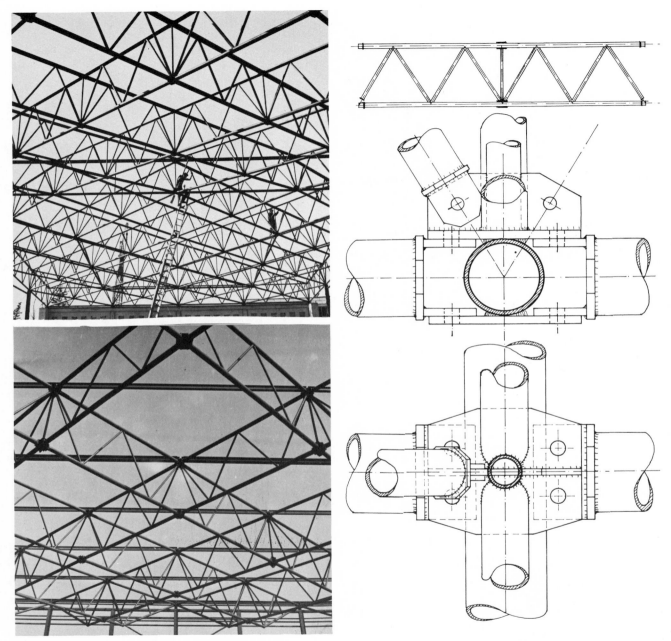

Plate 87
The TRIDIMATIC system by M. S. du Chateau. This is used in two-
and three-way lattice space grids. The TRIDIMATIC system was
developed as an alternative to the S.D.C. system. The choice was a
shop-welded, field-bolted system (TRIDIMATIC) versus a completely
field-welded system (S.D.C.) 1. View of a two-way lattice space
grid. 2. A two-way lattice space grid, diagonally braced. 3. Details
of the connection.

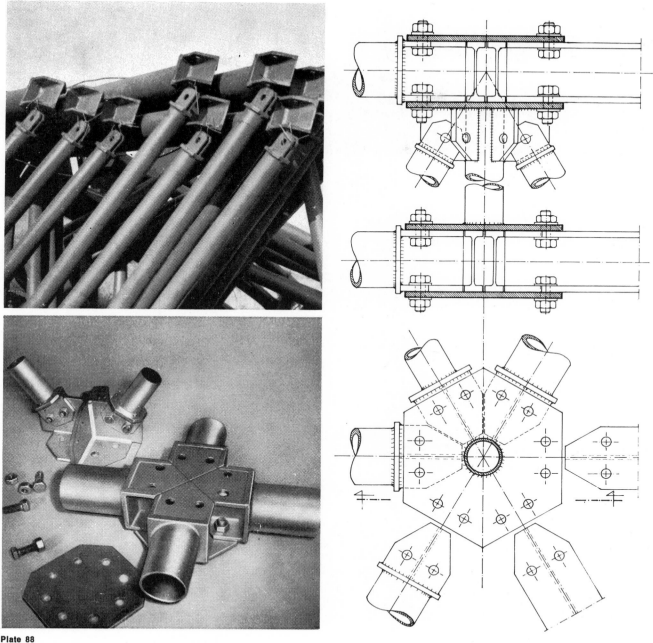

Plate 88
1. View of prefabricated elements of the TRIDIMATIC lattice space grid. 2. View of the two-way TRIDIMATIC connector and its components. 3. View of a TRIDIMATIC connector for a three-way lattice space grid.

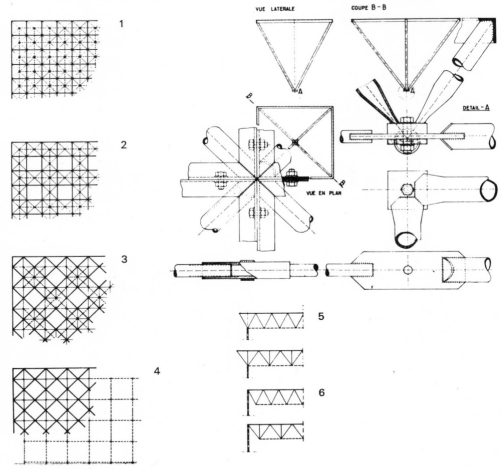

VUE LATERALE

COUPE B - B

DETAIL - A

VUE EN PLAN

1

2

3

4

5

6

Plate 89
PYRAMITEC, a three-dimensional (triangular, orthogonal, hexagonal) structural system, by M. S. du Chateau. This system consists of prefabricated three-dimensional pyramids. The pyramids consist of welded frames made of steel angles with steel tube diagonals connecting to an apex piece, which in turn receives the adjustable tie bars.
1. View of an orthogonal PYRAMITEC system. Possible grids, supporting conditions, top and bottom grid connection details of the orthogonal PYRAMITEC system.

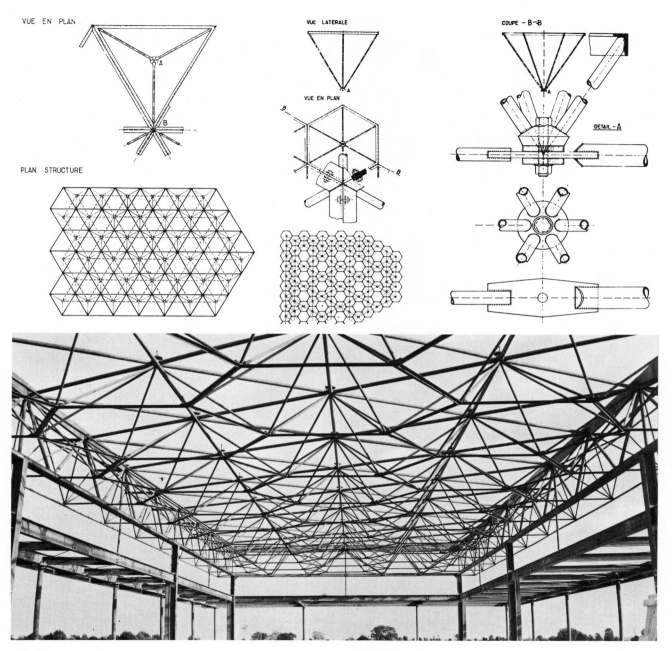

VUE EN PLAN

PLAN STRUCTURE

VUE LATERALE

VUE EN PLAN

COUPE – B–B

DETAIL – A

Plate 90
1. Triangular PYRAMITEC system and the resulting grid. 2. A hexagonal
PYRAMITEC system and the resulting grid, with details of the top
and bottom grid connections.

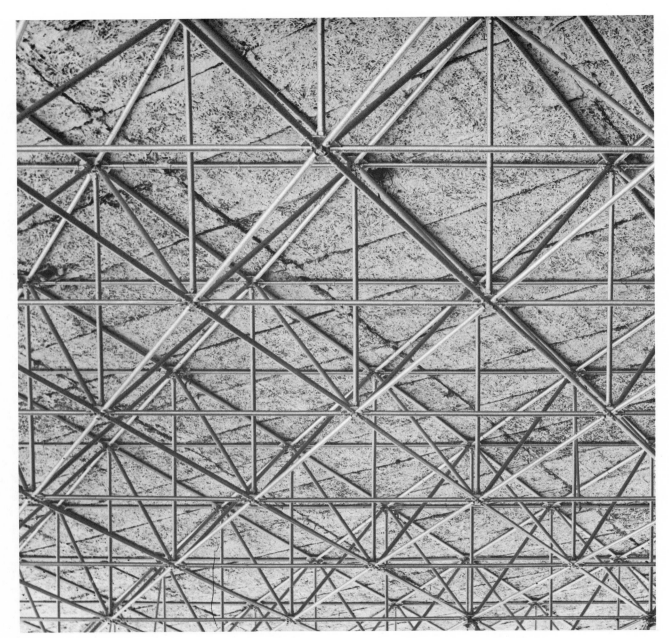

Plate 91
Project by Ignacio Alvarez Castelao for a service station at Oviedo, Spain. The owner wanted to build the station himself; the solution illustrated was evolved and may be adapted to two- and three-way space grids. The system consists of a disc with the necessary holes, according to the type of structure used, a tripod that varies according to the requirements, a tube with flutes and bore-holes at both ends, and two types of bolts—one to join the tripod and disc, the other to connect them with the tubes. The low weight of the parts permits assembly of the structure on the floor and subsequent elevation. 1. View of the three-way double-layer space grid.

Plate 92
1. The five basic elements of this system: disc, tripod, tube, and two sizes of bolts. 2. The five elements assembled into a node.

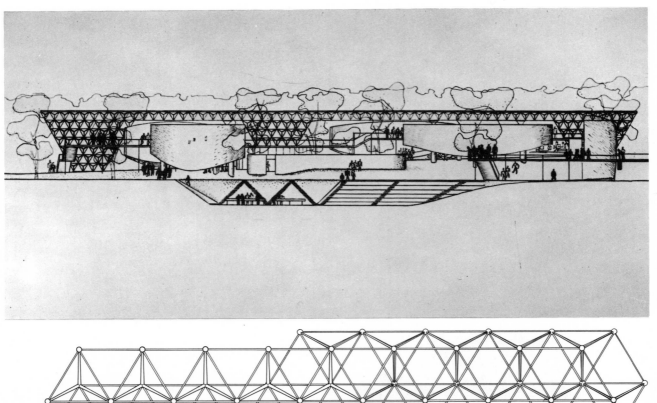

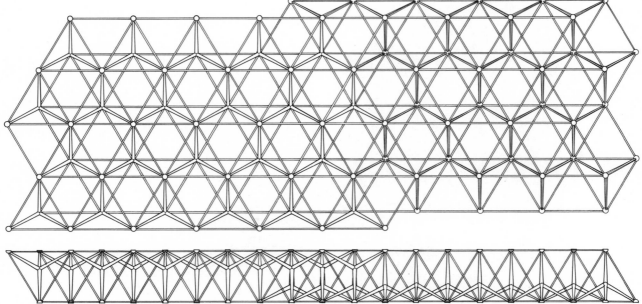

Plate 93
BX-58 grid, project by Jerzy W. Soltan Architect, Z. B. Ihnatowlcz, Architect, and Lech Tomaszewksi, Structural Engineer. The structure was developed for the Polish pavilion in the International Exhibition at Brussels in 1958. They tried to isolate the forces in the three-way grid and to resist tension by flexible rods and compression by precast reinforced concrete units. 1. Section through the pavilion. One sees the structural slab of the roof and supports. 2. Plan and elevation of the BX-58 grid illustrating the various layouts of the tripods, a progression from span (at left), over support (middle) and cantilever (at right).

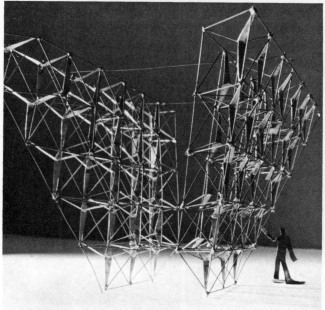

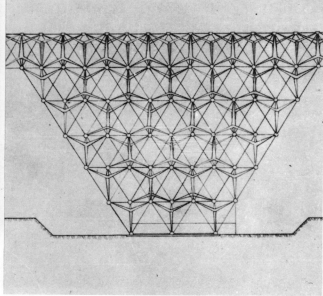

Plate 94

In the BX-58 grid the six bars forming the tetrahedron in a three-way space grid are replaced by flexible rods and stiffened by a rigid reinforced concrete tripod put inside the tetrahedron. The rods can be easily prestressed by means of turnbuckles or screws at the prefabricated hemispherical nodes. It is capable of considerable spans. 1. Structure erected in Warsaw for research. Concrete elements (cores) compressed; steel elements in tension; spherical joints. 2. Model of BX-58 grid at support. 3. Drawings of structural support.

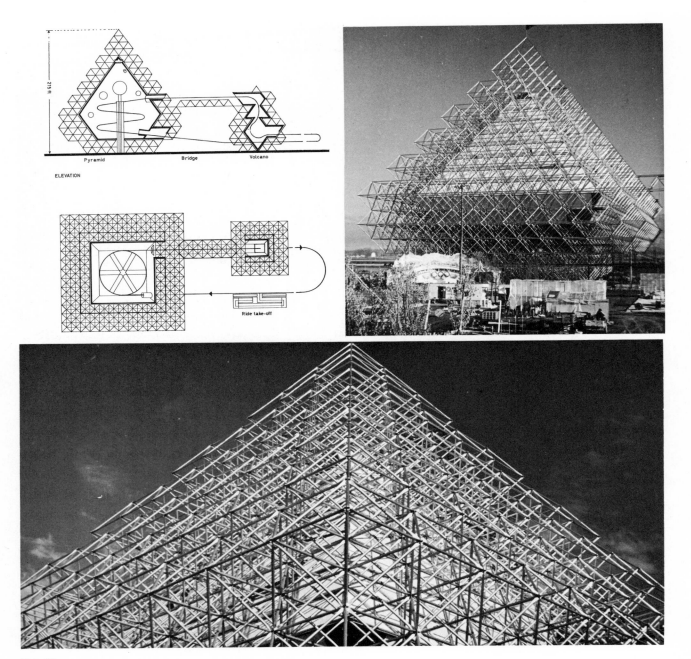

Plate 95
1. Elevation and general layout of the space frame exhibition structure designed by Boyd Auger for EXPO '67, Montreal. 2.–3. View of the completed structure. The members of the space frame are aluminum tubes between 5"-8" in diameter.

Plate 96
1. A close-up of one of the fabricated steel joints used in this structure.
2. Supporting point showing how the tubes are formed and joined to a base connector. 3. A close-up of the 16' long aluminum tubes that make up the structure.

Plate 97
Space frame exhibition structures for EXPO '67, Montreal. Architects: Affleck, Desbarats, Dimikopolus, Lebensold, Sise. Structural engineers: de Stein and Associates, Eskenazi and Baracs consulting. The structural system was to accommodate floor spans up to 125' with total loads up to 200 lb per sq ft. The structure allows a multiplicity of building shapes and sizes. The slabs of nested truncated tetrahedrons were used for roofs, floors, and walls. 1. Ile Notre Dame Complex. 2. Ile Verte Complex. 3. Erection of structural unit. 4. Structural unit nearing completion. 5. Typical wall section. Only chords and face bracing are shown.

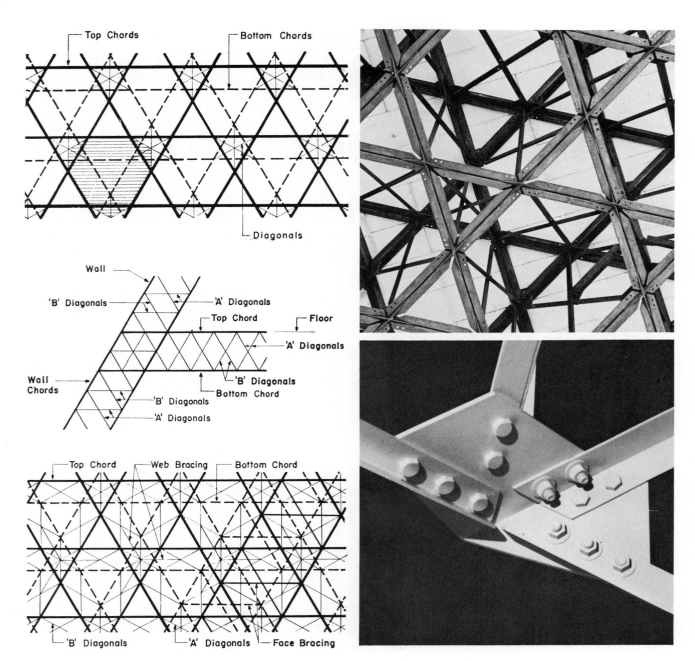

Plate 98
1. Plan of Vierendeel structure, basic cell shown hatched. 2. Section of floor and wall intersection. 3. Typical floor framing. 4. Detail of floor framing. 5. Model of node.

107

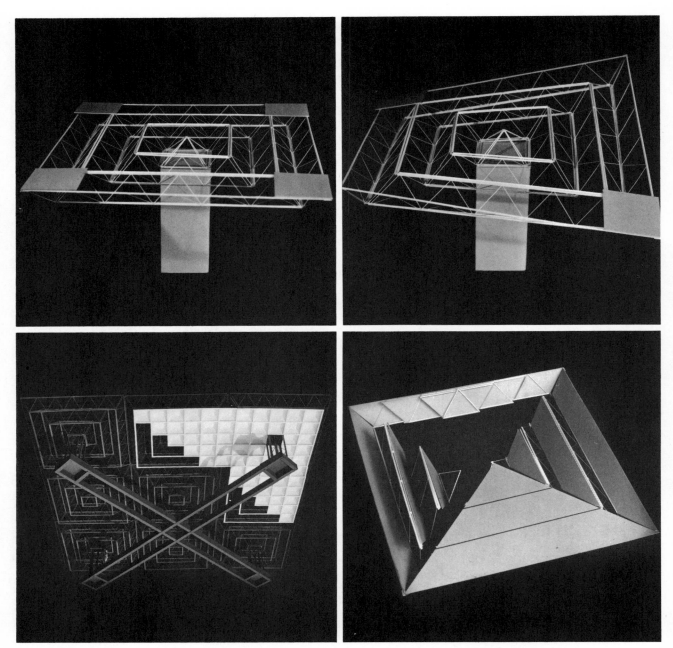

Plate 99
Project by Anthony E. Layton. M.Arch. Thesis at the Massachusetts Institute of Technology School of Architecture and Planning under Eduardo Catalano, 1965. The system is unique in that it eliminates the bracing members from the bottom chords, which are present in conventional space frames. 1. A symmetrically loaded structure transmits the loads inwards by a series of truss "rings" along the diagonals of the structural unit to the column. There are no horizontal forces in the structure, eliminating the need for an integral slab. 2. When asymmetrically loaded, this results in torsion creating a horizontal force. It is therefore necessary to use the floor integrally to close the section of the ring. The resulting structure is undergoing torsion by bending. 3. A combination of 9 concentric units. 4. Typical unit showing demountability of the system.

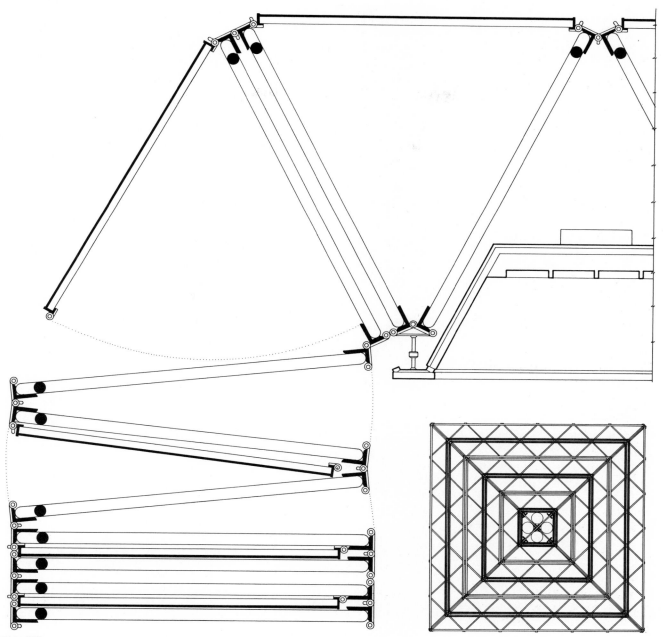

Plate 100
Assembly procedure. The trusses are bolted together by a system of hinges and bolted connections. The initial assembly process involved folding a set of trusses into a compact accordionlike package. These can then be shipped to the site, with the steel floor system sandwiched between them, unfolded, bolted together at the ends, and lifted into place. The procedure used to demount portions of the structure once the building is erected is to disengage each closed section of the ring at the hinges and to lower the sections separately to the floor below for further disassembly.

Part II
Stressed-Skin Space Grids

An improvement and extension of the skeleton type of double-layer grids is a stressed-skin sheet space grid system, which combines several advantages of the skeleton and sheet systems—great structural efficiency with many advantages of prefabrication.

In stressed-skin sheet structures, the compression edges of the sheet units receive additional lateral restraint from the adjacent sheets, preventing their tendency to buckle. Analytical studies and model investigations by Dr. Z. S. Makowski show that the load distribution is remarkably uniform. Sheet space systems depend mainly on shape, on the geometrical configurations, and only to a limited extent on the properties of the material of which such units are made. These structures are rigid; displacements do not control their design. The low Young's modulus, which may be a drawback in normal structural applications, is not so important in the case of stressed-skin space grids. These sheet structures can be made of materials that normally could not be used efficiently in structures of the conventional type because of their brittleness or low modulus of elasticity.

Aluminum, thin-gauge sheeting of steel, reinforced asbestos, or moulded plywood sheets can prove efficient and economical in the construction of the sheet structures. Plastics, which normally are not suitable for structural elements because of their low Young's modulus, can be used in stressed-skin space systems in which the stress distribution is membranal. In these systems, axial forces are of paramount importance, with virtual elimination of bending stresses.

Various tests have been carried out by Dr. Z. S. Makowski on full-size aluminum pyramids, using different thicknesses of sheets and investigating the effectiveness of welded, riveted, or glued connections. These tests revealed a surprisingly high load-carrying capacity of the pyramidal units, it being virtually impossible to produce a complete collapse. Even after "failure" the pyramid is still able to resist a very substantial percentage of the "collapse" load. See Bibliography for Dr. Z. S. Makowski's articles on stressed-skin structures.

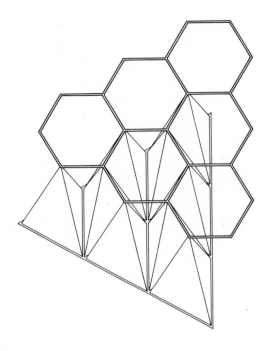

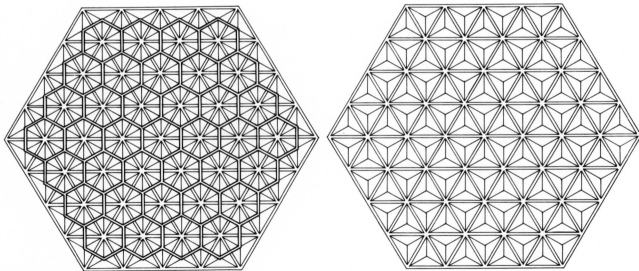

Plate 101
1. A stressed-skin space grid with tetrahedra on a triangular grid.
2. Plan of the interconnected apexes of the tetrahedra forming a hexagonal grid. 3. Plan looking up onto the tetrahedral pyramids. The interconnected flanges form a triangular grid.

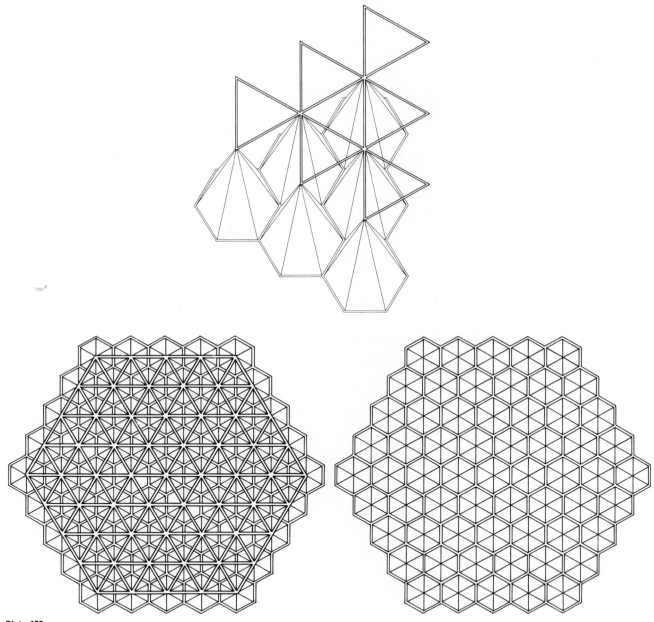

Plate 102
1. A stressed-skin space grid of hexagonal pyramids. 2. Plan of the interconnected apexes of the hexagonal pyramids forming a triangulated grid. 3. Plan looking up into the hexagonal pyramids. The interconnected flanges form the hexagonal grid.

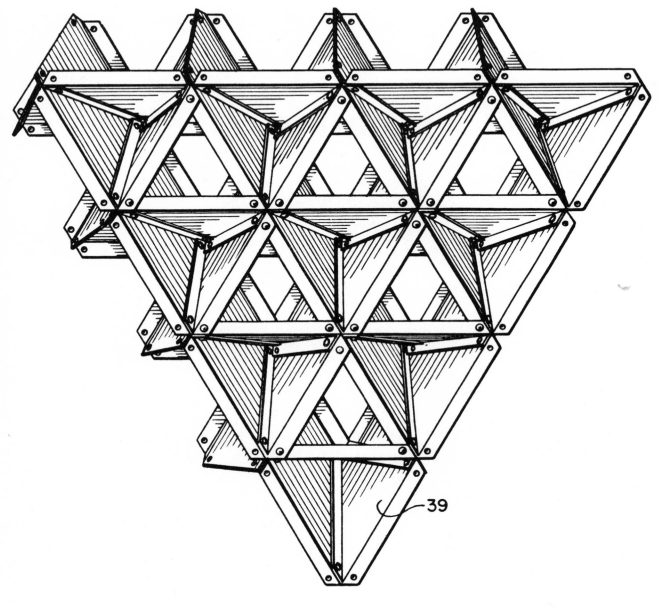

-39

FIG. 14

Plate 103
Project by Richard Buckminster Fuller. Fig. 14 is a top perspective
view of a stressed-skin, three-way, double-layer space grid made
from sheet modules, a modified form of the skeletal octetruss presented
on Plates 74 through 78. The truss is made up of identical modules,
just as the strut form of truss previously described. The flanges
of the modules may be fastened as shown or, in some cases, may
be held together with an epoxy cement.

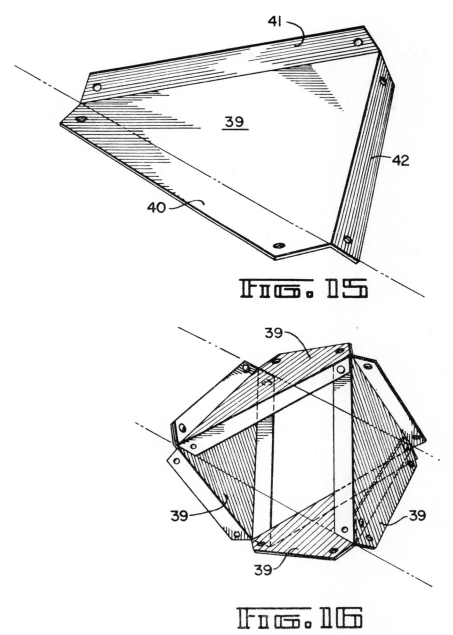

FIG. 15

FIG. 16

Plate 104
Fig. 15 is a perspective view of one of the sheets or plates that make up the octetruss. The sheets form an equilateral triangle. The flanges extend at an angle of approximately 109° 28'. Fig. 16 is a view of four plates assembled to form one of the octahedrons of the octetruss in Fig. 14.

Plate 105
A roof structure for the restaurant of the Bristol Hotel in Lagos, Nigeria. Project by Architects Co-Partnership, London. The structural design by Space Structures Research, Ltd., Z. S. Makowski structural consultant. The structure is 52′ × 48′, consisting of 150 aluminum pyramids and supported on four columns. The pyramid units are 4′ × 4′ at the base and 3′–6″ in height. 1. View looking up at the structure. The apexes of the pyramids are interconnected by prefabricated tie members forming a bottom-layer grid of a regular pattern. The flanges of the inverted pyramids are then fixed to the roof sheeting, closing the pyramids and bracing them in the horizontal plane. 2. Plan and section. 3. Die-cast apex connector, showing "cast-in" bolts.

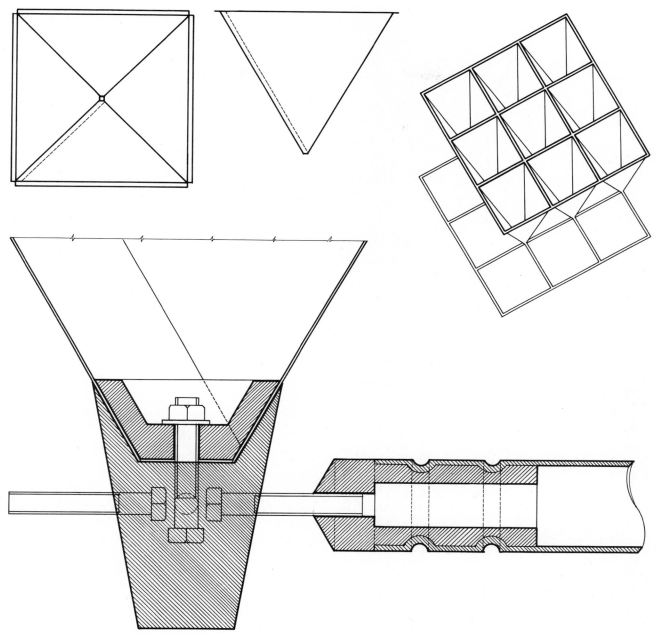

Plate 106
1. Plan and elevation of the typical pyramid used in the roof. 2. An isometric showing the stressed-skin system with the top grid made of interconnected flanges that are riveted together. The lower apexes are interconnected by a two-way grid of aluminum tubes. 3. Section of the apex connection, connecting the aluminum sheet pyramid and the tie rods of the bottom grid. The two gravity-die-cast parts are connected to a tie rod junction piece by "cast-in" ½" diameter bolts.

117

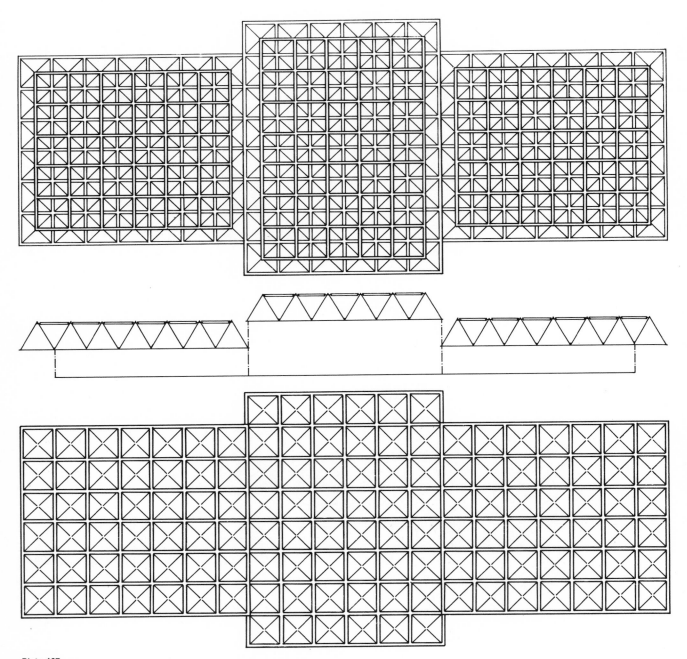

Plate 107
Building for the International Union of Architects Congress, 1961.
Project by Theo Crosby. The structural design by Space Structures
Research, Ltd., Z. S. Makowski structural consultant. Plan and elevation
and reflected ceiling of the two-way stressed-skin space grid. The
roof consists of 132 prefabricated aluminum pyramids, described
in Plate 108.

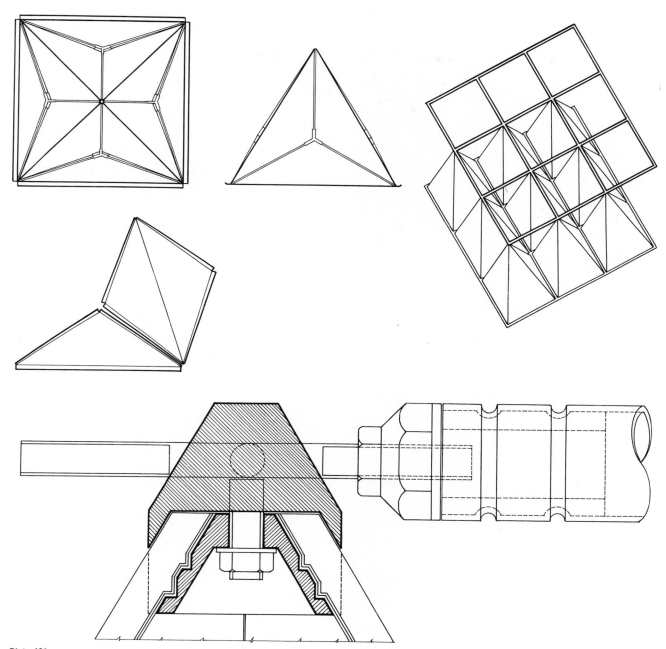

Plate 108
1. The plan, elevation, and components of the standard pyramid unit. The individual pyramids of 20-gauge aluminum are 8′ × 8′ at the base and 7′ in height. 2. Isometric of the stressed-skin system. The interconnection of the flanges is obtained by gluing with an Araldite epoxy resin. 3. Section of the apex connector connecting the aluminum sheet pyramid and the top grid. The 2 gravity-die-cast parts are connected to a tie rod junction piece by "cast in" bolts.

Plate 109
The reflected ceiling plan of the roof for the church at Dunstable,
England, by Arthur Farebrother and Partners. Structural design by
Space Structures Research, Ltd., Z. S. Makowski, structural consultant.
The roof has 12 segments each made up of 64 elongated tetrahedra.
Details on Plate 110.

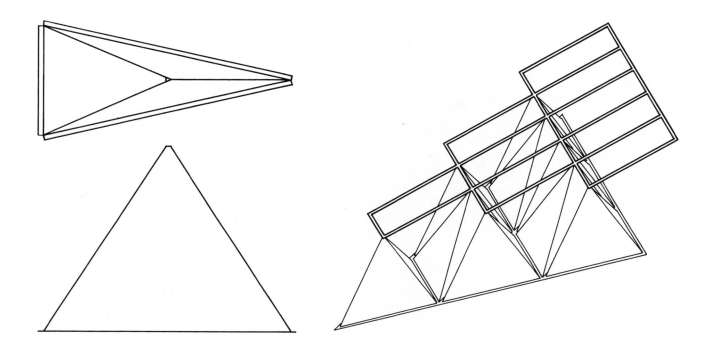

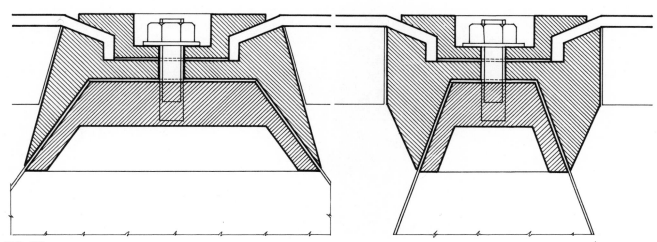

Plate 110
1. Plan and elevation of the typical pyramid used in the roof. 2. An isometric showing stressed-skin space grid with the top grid (rectilinear) made by interconnecting the apexes of the elongated tetrahedra. The riveted flanges of the pyramids form the triangular bottom grid.
3. Connector for the roof of the church at Dunstable, which fixes the upper grid simultaneously with the sheet sides of the pyramid.

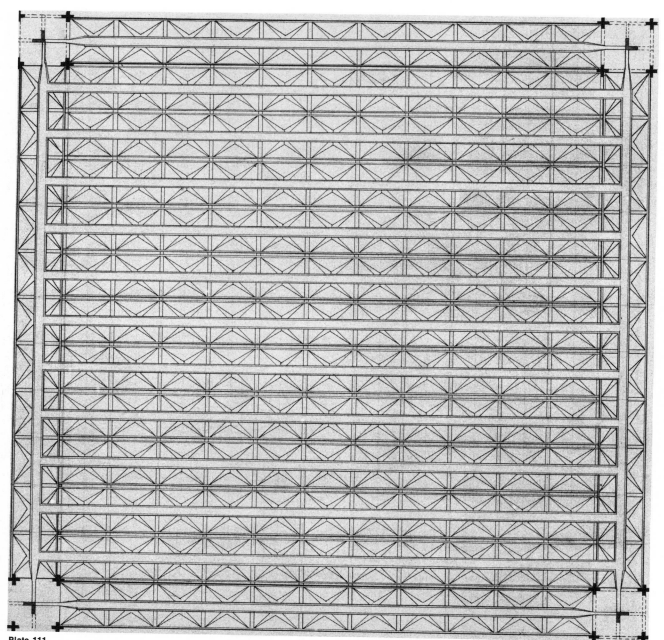

Plate 111
Project by Charles Lozar, M.Arch. Thesis at the Massachusetts Institute
of Technology under Eduardo Catalano and Waclaw Zalewski, 1965.
The structure is based on sheet steel elements that form linear
stressed-skin space trusses, which are interconnected to form the
structural bays.

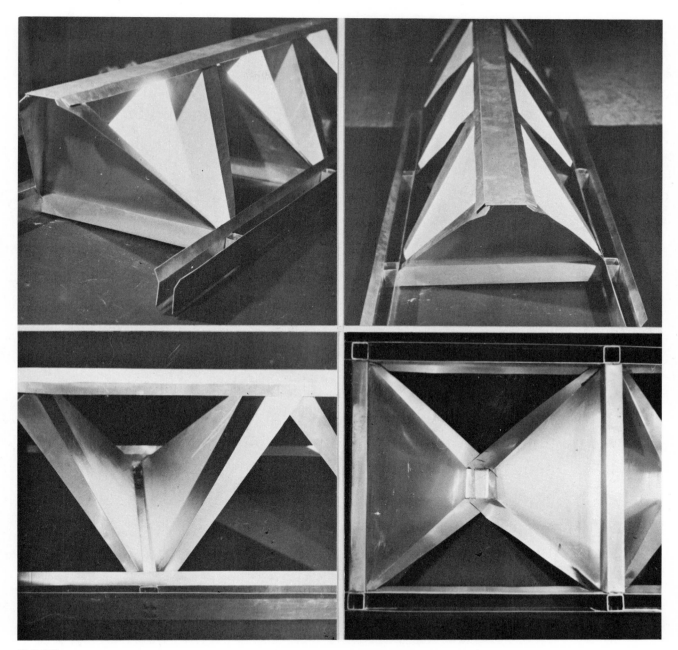

Plate 112
The trusses illustrated are made from sheets that form five edges of a
tetrahedron. The tetrahedral units are interconnected at the base to
form square-based pyramids. A linear element ties together the
apexes of the pyramids completing the truss.

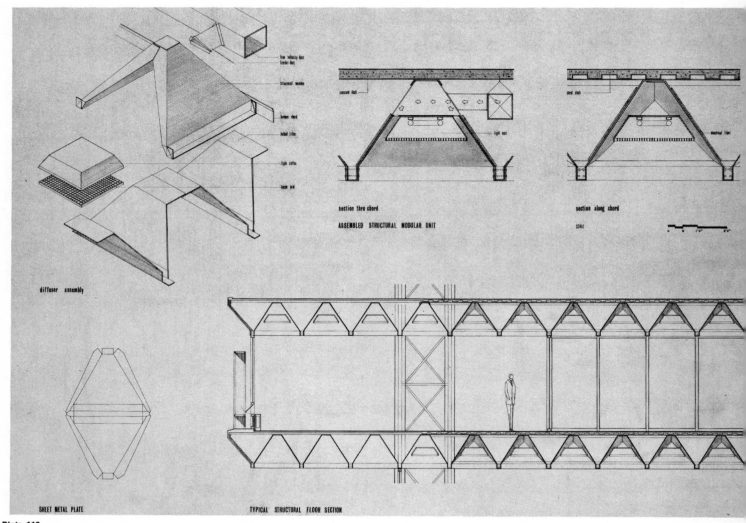

low velocity duct
feeder duct

diagonal member

bottom chord

folded trellis

light coffer

beam grid

diffuser assembly

concrete deck

light mat

section thru chord

ASSEMBLED STRUCTURAL MODULAR UNIT

steel deck

neutral trim

section along chord

SCALE

SHEET METAL PLATE

TYPICAL STRUCTURAL FLOOR SECTION

Plate 113
Plate 114
Details of the stressed-skin system showing the sheet metal plate,
assembled structural modular unit, detail of column, structural isometric,
structural connector, and a typical structural floor section.

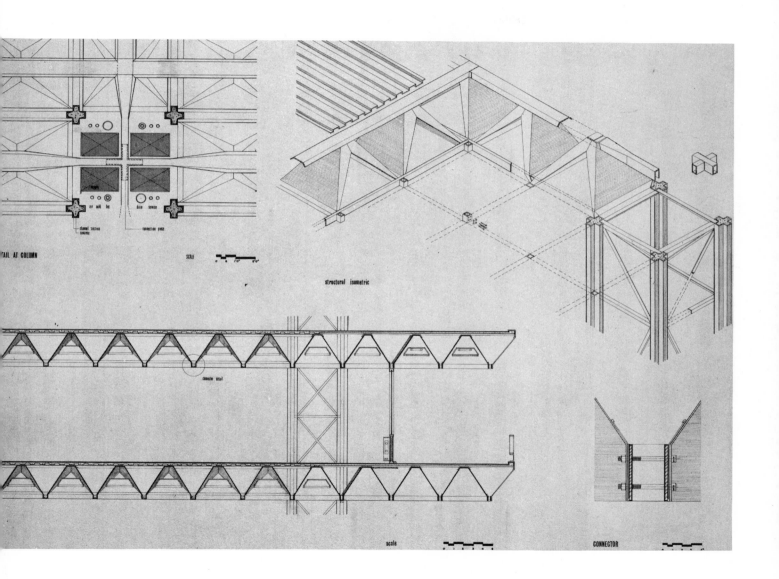

DETAIL AT COLUMN   SCALE

channel lacing
concrete   connection piece

structural isometric

connector detail

scale

CONNECTOR

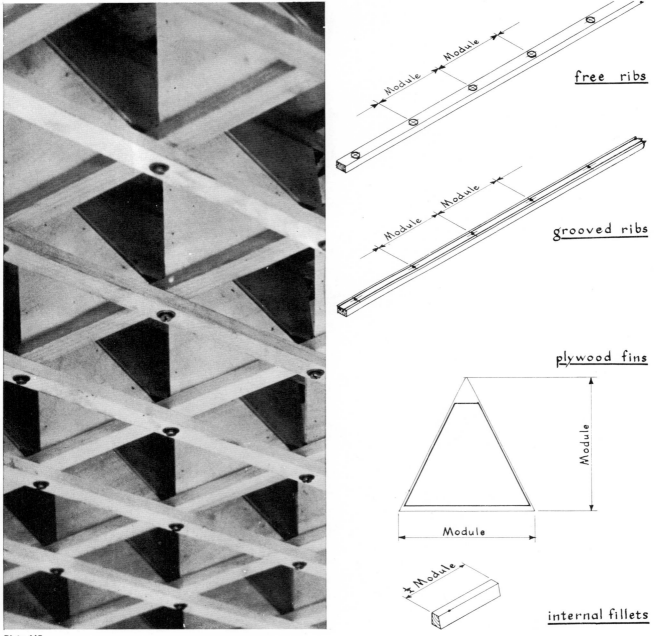

free ribs

grooved ribs

plywood fins

Module

Module

internal fillets

Module

Plate 115
TETRAGRID space frames by L. C. Booth and B. T. Keay. 1. View of the TETRAGRID space frame system. 2. Components of the TETRAGRID free rib, grooved rib, plywood fins, and internal fillets.

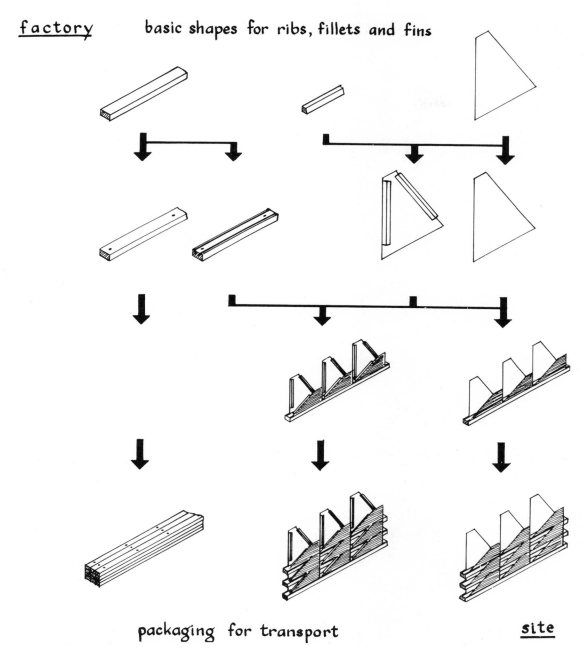

factory   basic shapes for ribs, fillets and fins

packaging for transport   site

Plate 116
Prefabrication of the TETRAGRID to form the units to be taken to
the site. "The ribs are drilled and grooved to take a split-ring connector,
and a standard jog is used to nail and glue the fillets to the fins.
The final factory operation is to slot the plywood fins into the grooved
ribs and to glue them into position." The plain ribs and grooved
ribs with fins are transported to the site.

assembly on site

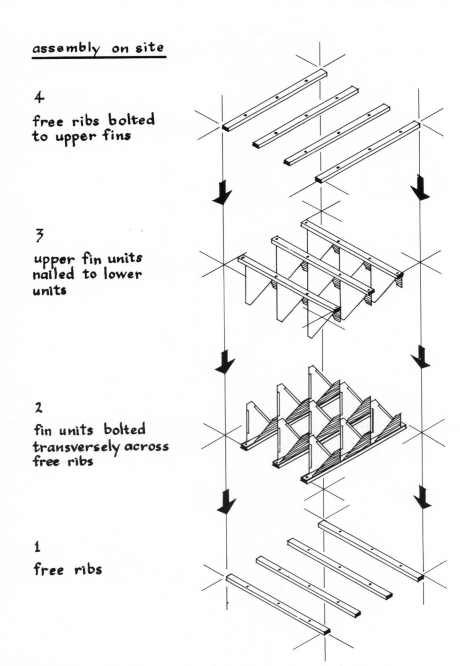

4

free ribs bolted
to upper fins

3

upper fin units
nailed to lower
units

2

fin units bolted
transversely across
free ribs

1

free ribs

Plate 117
Assembly of TETRAGRID on site. The order of combination is predetermined. There are, however, two possible erection methods: "The free ribs may be supported on a minimum of scaffolding or the roof may be assembled on the ground and lifted into position." "The free ribs carry the main tension and compression stresses in the space frame. The grooved ribs have the same structural function as the free ribs, but in addition form a continuous member common to a row of tetrahedrons. The plywood fins, fit into the grooved ribs to form the sides of the tetrahedrons and structurally resist shear stresses. The internal fillets act as jointing members along the edges of the tetrahedrons."

Tetragrid with free ribs. open construction

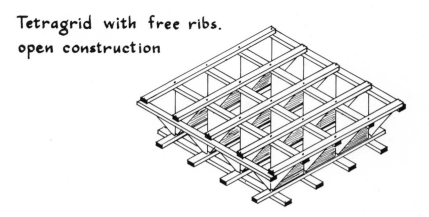

Tetragrid with stressed-skin plywood top deck

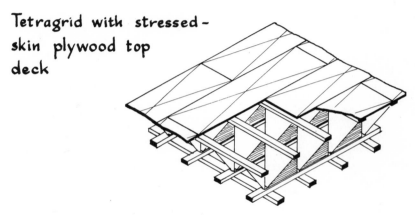

Tetragrid with stressed-skin plywood top deck and soffit

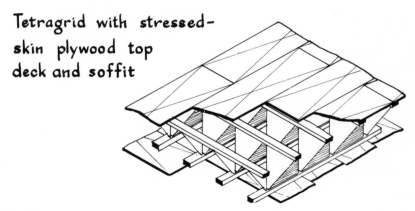

Plate 118
Variations of the TETRAGRID. 1. Free ribs on top and bottom. 2. Replace the top set of free ribs with stressed-skin sheets of plywood. 3. To produce a completely stressed-skin system, replace both sets of free ribs with plywood.

Part III
Space Grid Geometries

An outline of the space grid geometries will be presented in this section. Because single-layer grids form the basis for most double-layer grids, we will look at the various regular and semiregular polygons which will give us single-layer grids with equal-length elements. These polygons, except the triangle, when used structurally, must be held rigid either by division into triangles or by the use of a stressed-skin membrane.

The following have the two-way symmetry of the square:
1. Square
2. Right-hand triangle-square
3. Left-hand triangle-square
4. Alternating triangle-square
5. Octagon-square

The square, triangle, and hexagon form the only three regular tessellations in which all the polygons are identical. These polygons provide the most simple geometries for the space grids, resulting in a system with a few simple repetitive elements which simplify fabrication.

Other single-layer grids, not all having equal-length elements:

Two-way symmetry

14. Rectangular
15. Skewed

Three-way symmetry

16. Diagonally braced square
17. Diagonally braced rectangle

Four-way symmetry

18. Square
19. Rectangular
20. Diagonally braced square
21. Diagonally braced rectangle

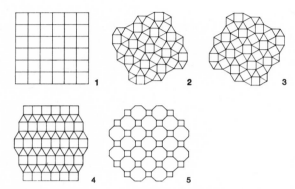

The following possess the three-way symmetry of the triangle and hexagon:

6. Triangle
7. Lesser triangle-hexagon
8. Right-hand greater triangle-hexagon
9. Left-hand greater triangle-hexagon
10. Hexagon
11. Triangle-dodecagon
12. Triangle-square-hexagon
13. Square-hexagon-dodecagon

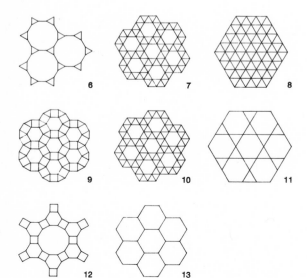

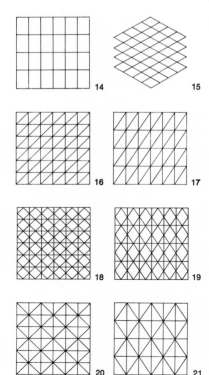

Double-layer space grids consist of two single-layer grids spaced apart and interconnected by bracing members. The upper and lower grids can be arranged in the following ways:

1. *Direct Grid.* Two grids similar in design, with one layer directly over the top of the other—thus both grids are directionally the same. Upper and lower grids are connected by bracing.

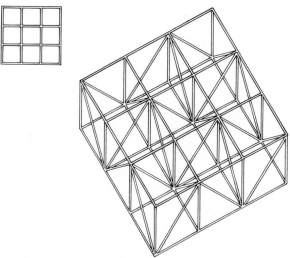

2. *Offset Grid.* Two grids, similar in geometry, with one grid offset from the other in plan but remaining directionally the same. The upper and lower grids are connected by bracing.

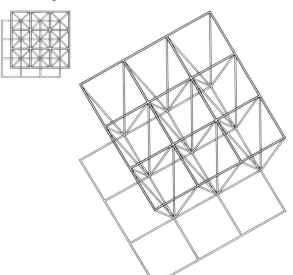

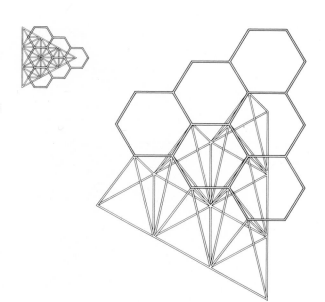

3. *Differential Grid.* Two grids that may be different in design and are therefore directionally different but chosen to co-ordinate and form a regular pattern. Upper and lower grids are interconnected by bracing. When specifying the types of grids, the top grid is stated first.

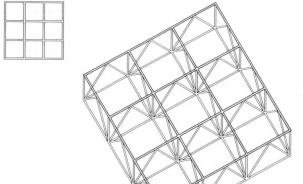

4. *Lattice Grid.* This is a double-layer space grid that has upper and lower members braced to form a girder prior to erection. The girders are assemblies prefabricated in the workshop. In this type of assembly, the upper and lower members are placed close together and, when braced, may be considered a stiffened single-layer space grid. In all other respects it is similar to the direct grid.

INDEX TO SPACE GRID GEOMETRIES*

	Two-Way					Three-Way	
	Square / Rectangular	Skewed	Right Triangle-Square / Left Triangle-Square	Alternating Triangle-Square	Octagon Square	Triangle	Less Triangle-H
DIRECT	169 179	174 179	179	179	179	175 179	17
OFFSET	119–126 129–130 180	180				159–162	
DIFFERENTIAL	127–128 143–146		180	180	139–140 143–146 180	147–158 163–166 180	18 165– 1
LATTICE	133–134 169–170 179	174 179	179	179	177 179	175 179	1 1

*Plate numbers are given.

Three-Way						Four-Way	
Greater Hexagon reater Hexagon	Hexagon	Triangle-Dodecagon	Triangle-Square-Hexagon	Square-Hexagon-Dodecagon	Diagonally Braced Square Diagonally Braced Rectangle	Square Differential Rectangular Differential	Diagonally Braced Square Diagonally Braced Rectangle
79	176 179	179	179	179	179	131–132 179	131–132 179
	167–168				137–138	180	
65 80	147–158 163–166 180	180	180	180	135–136 180	141–142	139–140 180
178 179	176 179	179	179	179	171 179	133–134 173 179	171–172 179

Row labels (right margin): DIRECT, OFFSET, DIFFERENTIAL, LATTICE

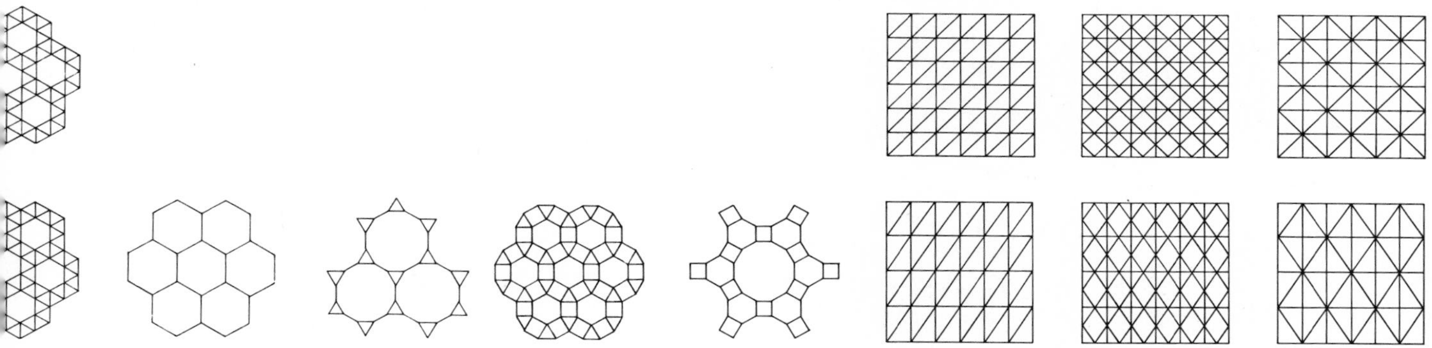

The initial study of space grid geometries was conducted as follows: A grid had pyramids placed on each described polygon, the apexes were connected, and the resulting geometry was recorded. Then pyramid modules were removed, resulting in systems with internal openings that were still stable and/or capable of lighter loading. This was done for other two-, three-, and four-way grids. This study describes but a few of the many possibilities suggested in the matrix shown.

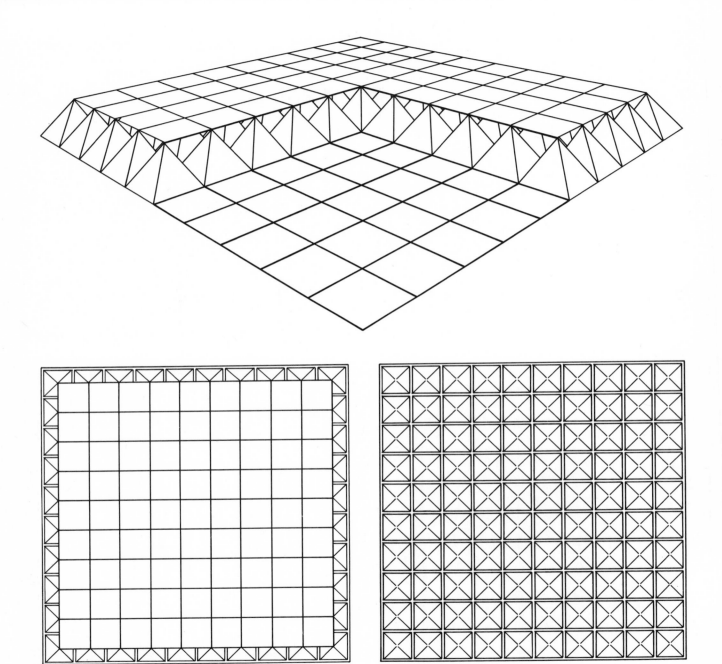

Plate 119
1. Perspective of a stressed-skin space grid with pentahedrons on an orthogonal grid. 2. Top grid. 3. Bottom grid.

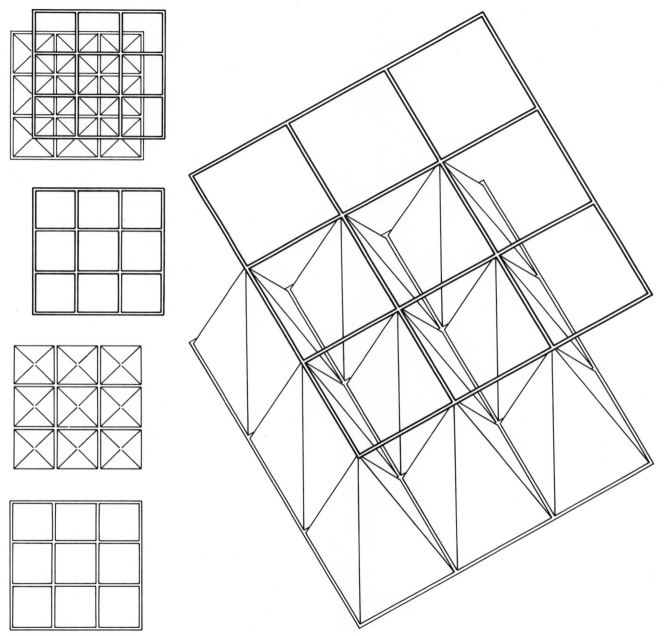

Plate 120

1. Orthogonal stressed-skin space grid. *Component parts:* 2. Top grid formed by interconnected apexes of pyramids. 3. Pyramids' inclined edges and surfaces provide the diagonal webbing. 4. Bottom. grid formed by the interconnected bases of the pyramids. 5. Isometric of the network.

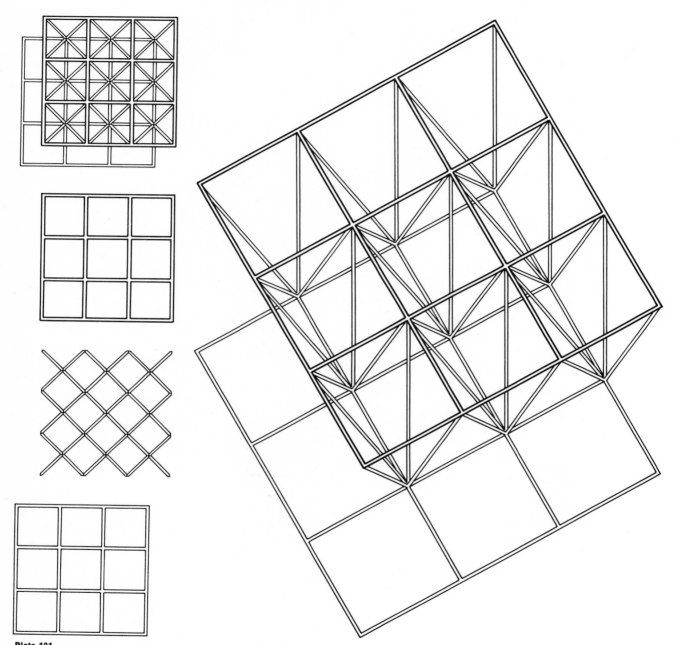

Plate 121
1. A skeletal space grid with the top and bottom grid interconnected by diagonal web members forming alternating pentahedrons and tetrahedrons. *Component parts:* 2. Top grid. 3. Diagonal web members. 4. Bottom grid. 5. Isometric of the network.

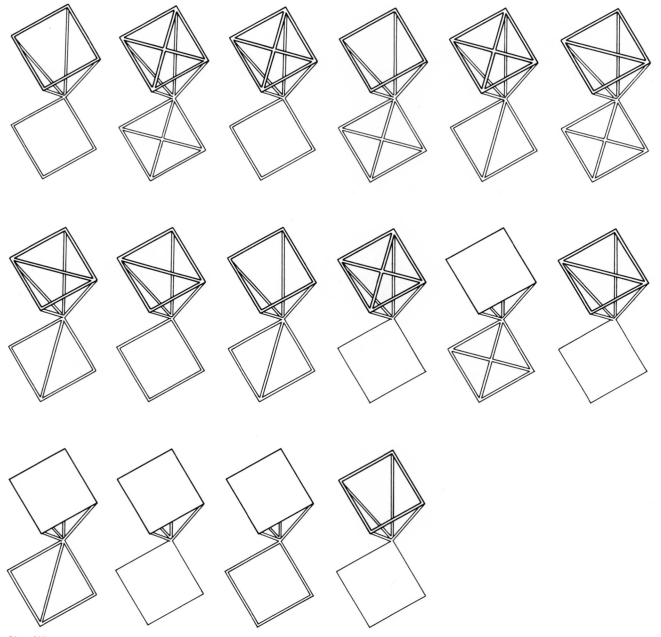

Plate 122
Combination of members or surfaces used to stabilize the top and bottom grids in various orthogonal skeletal space grids.

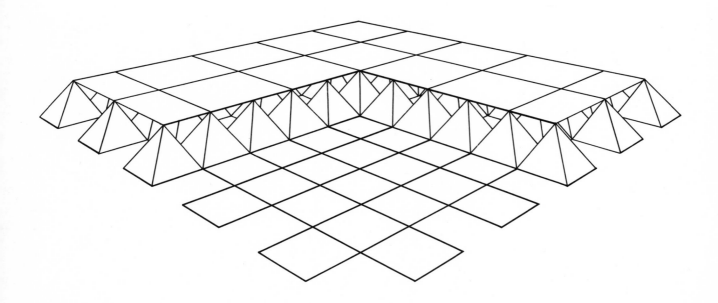

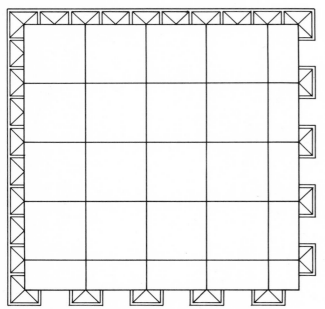

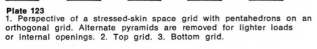

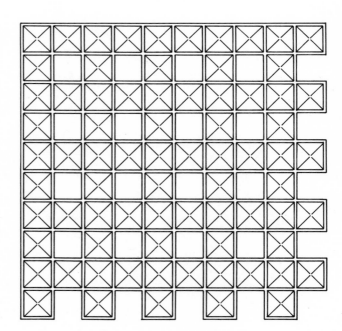

Plate 123
1. Perspective of a stressed-skin space grid with pentahedrons on an orthogonal grid. Alternate pyramids are removed for lighter loads or internal openings. 2. Top grid. 3. Bottom grid.

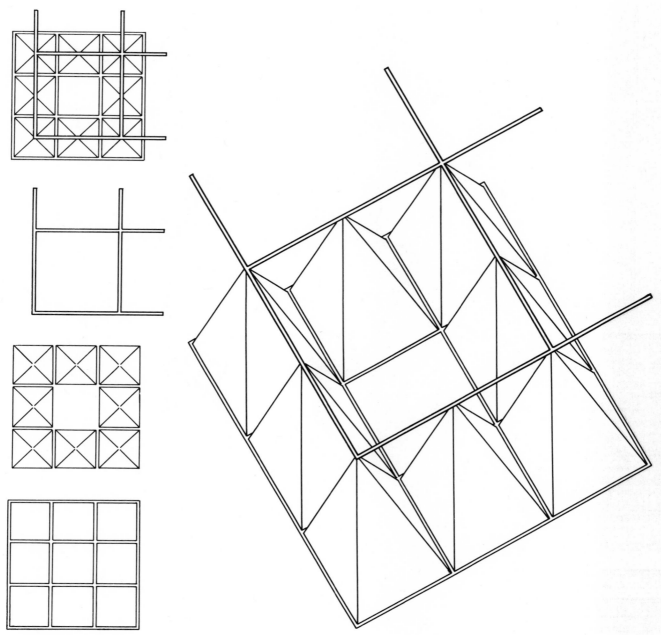

Plate 124
1. Orthogonal stressed-skin space grid with internal openings. *Component parts:* 2. Top grid formed by interconnected apexes of pyramids.
3. Pyramids' inclined edges and surfaces provide the diagonal webbing.
4. Bottom grid formed by the interconnected bases of the pyramids.
5. Isometric of the network.

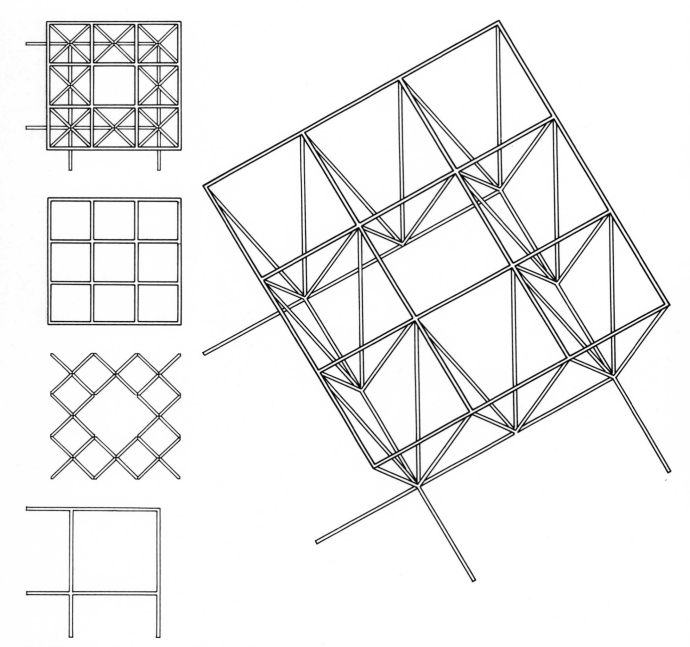

Plate 125
1. An orthogonal skeletal space grid with internal opening. *Component parts*: 2. Top grid. 3. Diagonal web members. 4. Bottom grid. 5. Isometric of the network.

142

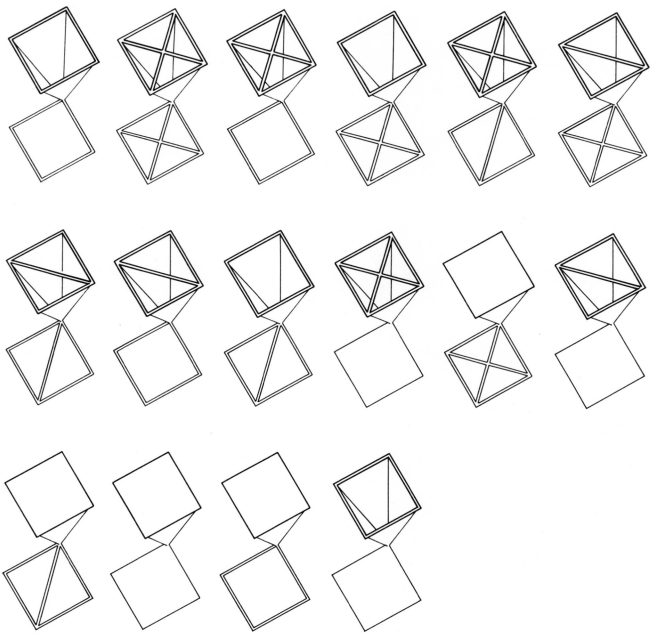

Plate 126
Combinations of members or surfaces used to stabilize the top and
bottom grids in various orthogonal stressed-skin space grids.

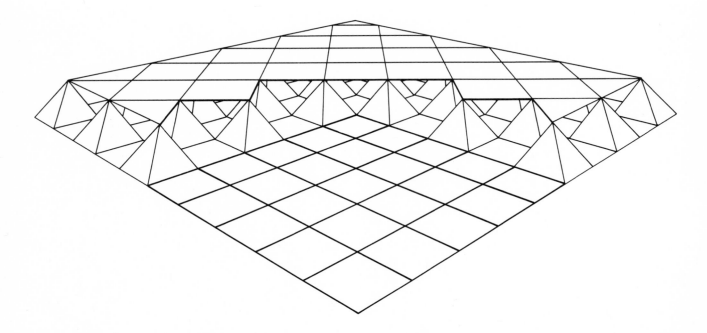

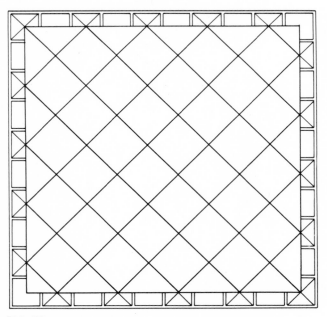

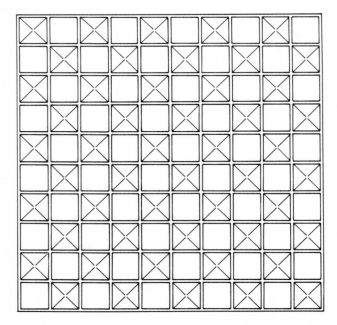

Plate 127
1. Perspective of a stressed-skin space grid with pentahedrons on an orthogonal grid. Alternate pyramids are removed for lighter loads or internal openings. The top grid is a diagonal grid with a triangulated edge condition, which is stronger than the orthogonal network.
2. Top grid. 3. Bottom grid.

144

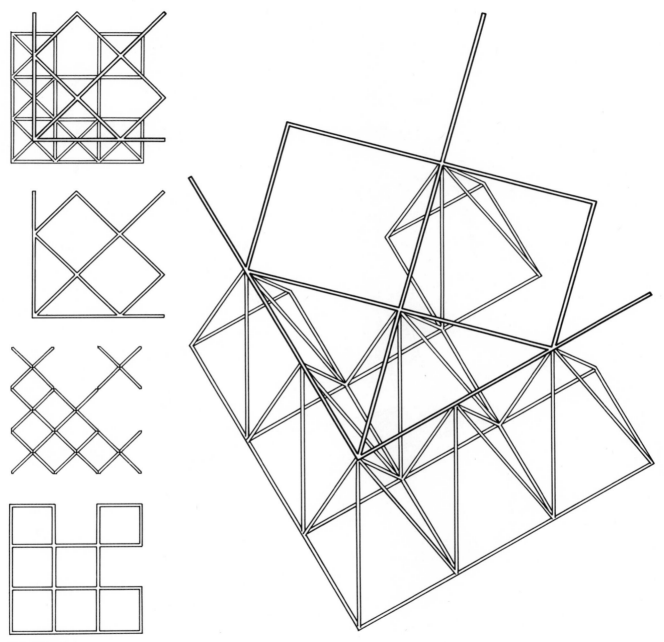

Plate 128
1. An orthogonal skeletal space grid with internal openings. The top grid is diagonal. *Component parts:* 2. Top grid. 3. Diagonal web members. 4. Bottom grid. 5. Isometric of the network.

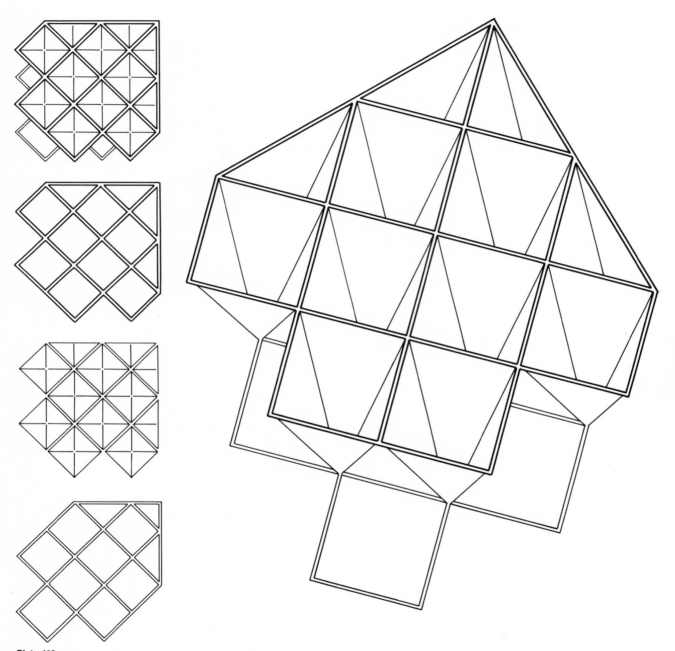

Plate 129

1. A diagonal stressed-skin space grid with pentahedrons on a grid turned 45° to the edge. The top and bottom grids have a triangulated edge condition. *Component parts:* 2. Top grid formed by interconnected bases of the pyramids. 3. Pyramids' inclined surfaces and edges provide the diagonal webbing. 4. Bottom grids formed by the interconnected apexes of the pyramids. 5. Isometric of the network.

146

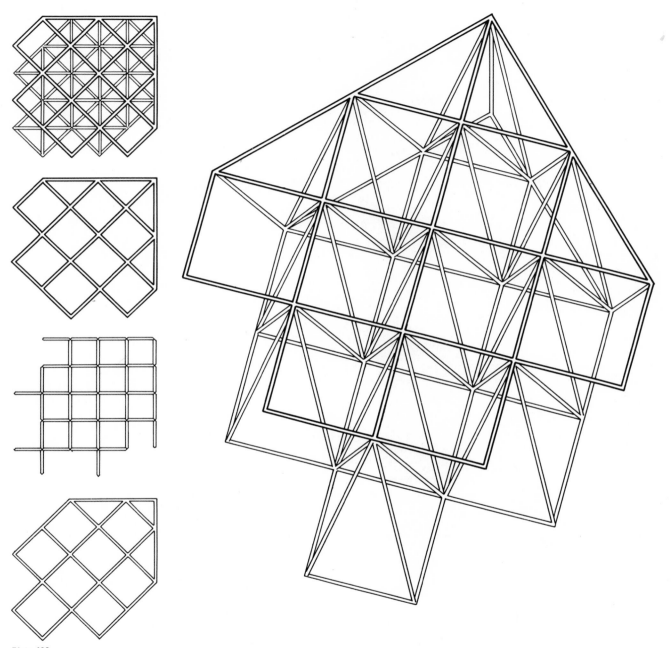

Plate 130
1. A diagonal skeletal space grid with top and bottom diagonal grids interconnected by diagonal web members forming alternating pentahedrons and tetrahedrons. *Component parts:* 2. Top grid. 3. Diagonal web members. 4. Bottom grid. 5. Isometric of network.

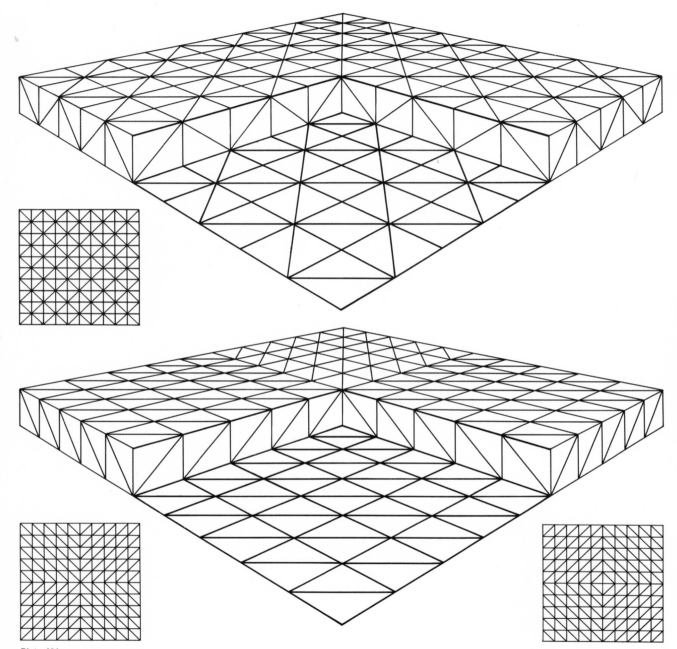

Plate 131
1.—2. Perspectives of the two variations of an orthogonal space grid
with the basic cell being the tetrahedral subdivision of the cube.

148

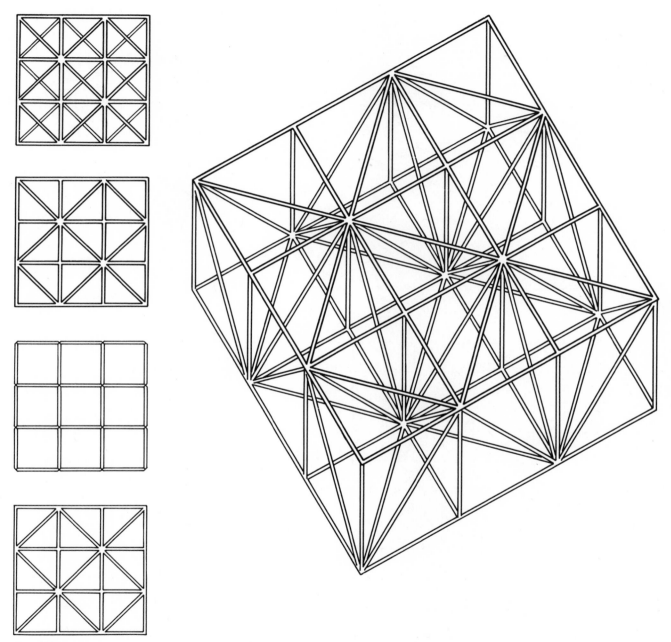

Plate 132
1. Orthogonal skeletal space grid. Tetrahedral subdivision of a cube.
Component parts: 2. Top grid. 3. Diagonal and vertical web members.
4. Bottom grid. 5. Isometric of network.

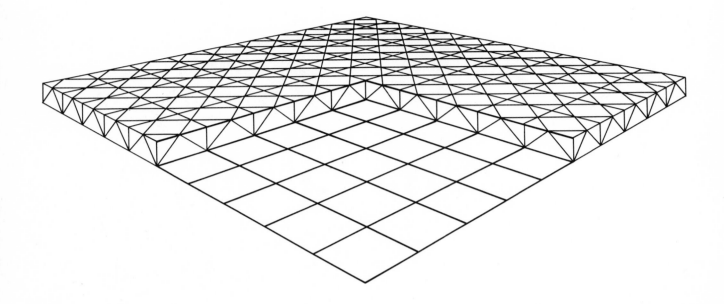

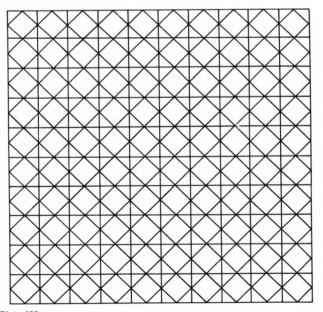

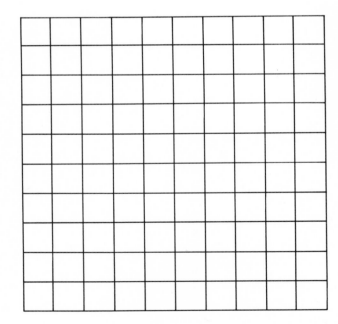

Plate 133
1. Perspective of orthogonal skeletal space grid. The basic cell is a
rectangular prism with right triangular tetrahedrons at each of the four
corners. 2. Top grid. 3. Bottom grid.

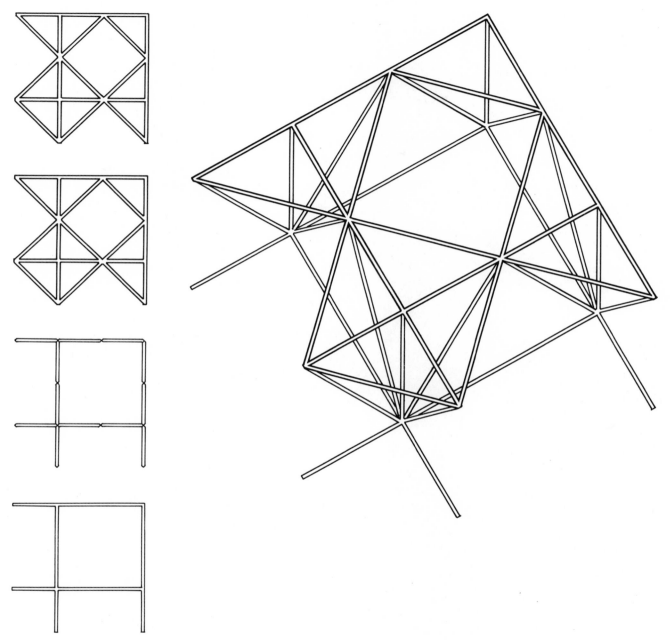

Plate 134
1. Orthogonal skeletal space grid. *Component parts:* 2. Top grid.
3. Diagonal and vertical web members. 4. Bottom grid. 5. Isometric
of network.

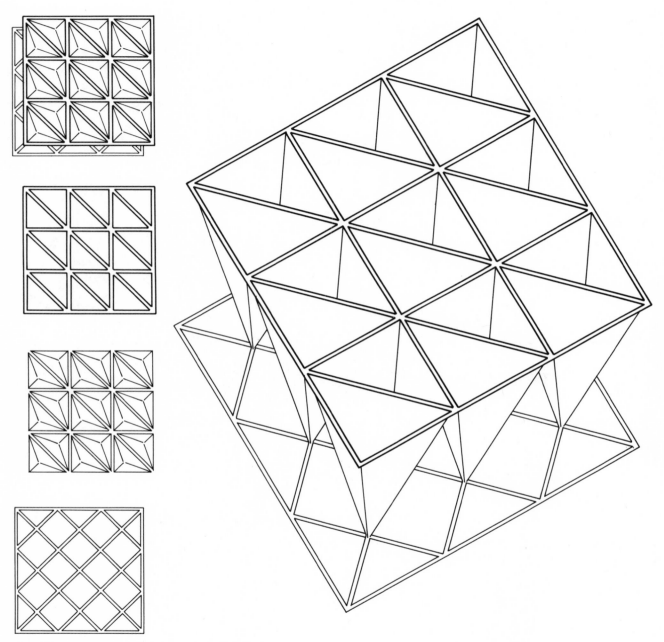

Plate 135
1. A stressed-skin space grid of right triangular-based pyramids.
Component parts: 2. Top grid formed by right triangular-based pyramids.
3. Pyramids' inclined edges and surfaces provide the diagonal webbing.
4. Bottom grid formed by interconnected apexes of the pyramids.
5. Isometric of the network.

152

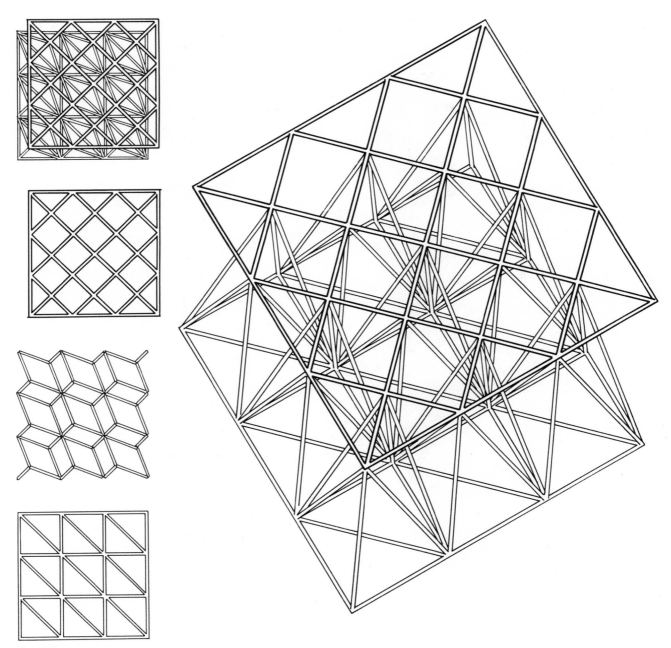

Plate 147
Perspective of a stressed-skin space grid with tetrahedrons on a
triangular grid with a rectangular periphery. 2. Top grid. 3. Bottom grid.

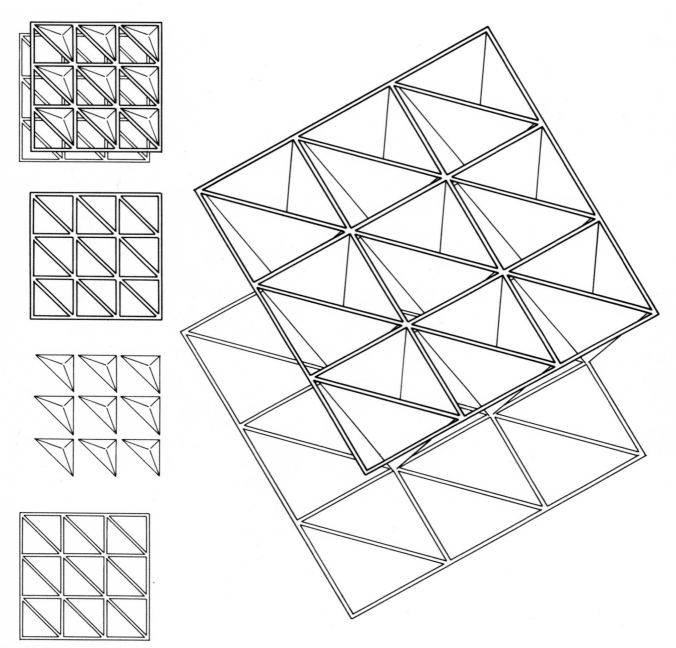

Plate 137
1. A stressed-skin space grid of right triangular-based pyramids with alternate pyramids removed resulting in a skewed triangular system. *Component parts:* 2. Top grid formed by interconnected pyramid bases. 3. Right triangular-based pyramids' inclined edges and surfaces provide the diagonal webbing. 4. Bottom grid formed by interconnected apexes of the pyramids. 5. Isometric of the network.

154

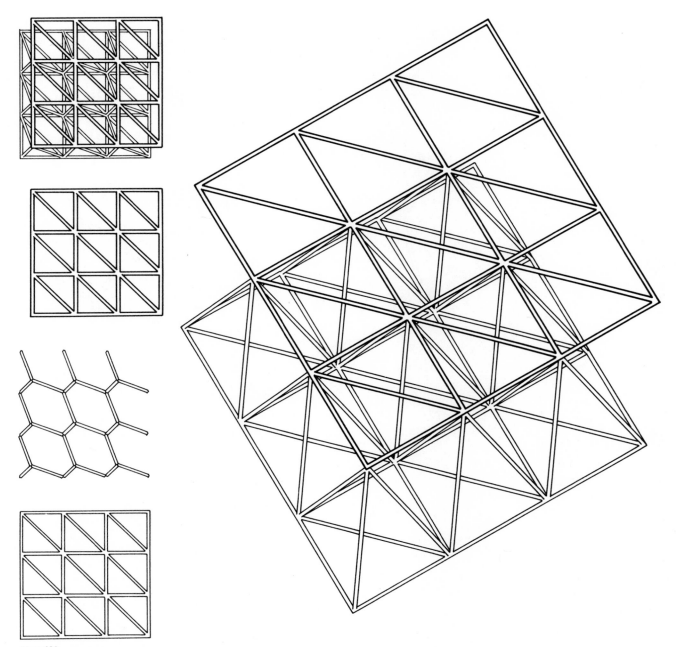

Plate 138
1. A skeletal space grid of right triangular top and bottom grids interconnected by diagonal web members to form alternating octahedra and tetrahedra. (A skewed three-way space grid.) *Component parts:* 2. Top grid of right triangles. 3. Diagonal web members. 4. Bottom grid of right triangles. 5. Isometric of network.

155

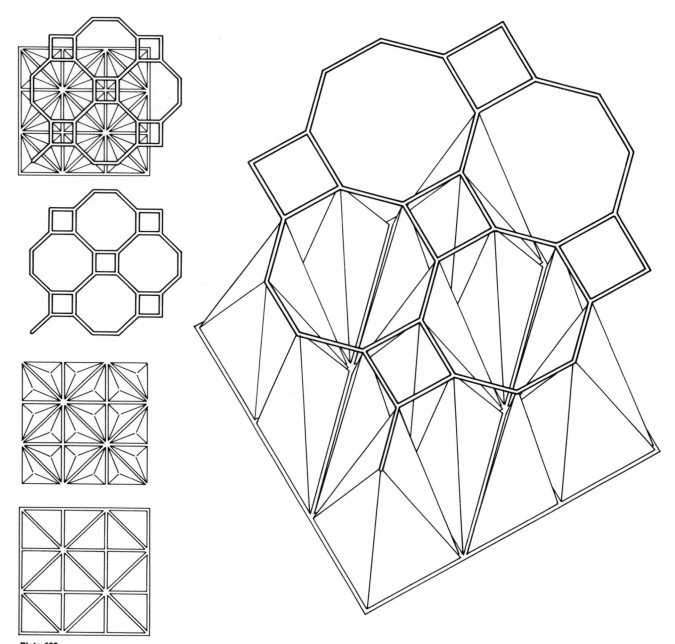

Plate 139
1. A stressed-skin space grid of right triangular-based pyramids.
Component parts: 2. Top grid formed by interconnected apexes of
pyramids, alternating octagons and squares. 3. Right triangular-based
pyramids' edges and surfaces provide the diagonal webbing. 4. Bottom
grid formed by the interconnected bases of the pyramids. 5. Isometric
of network.

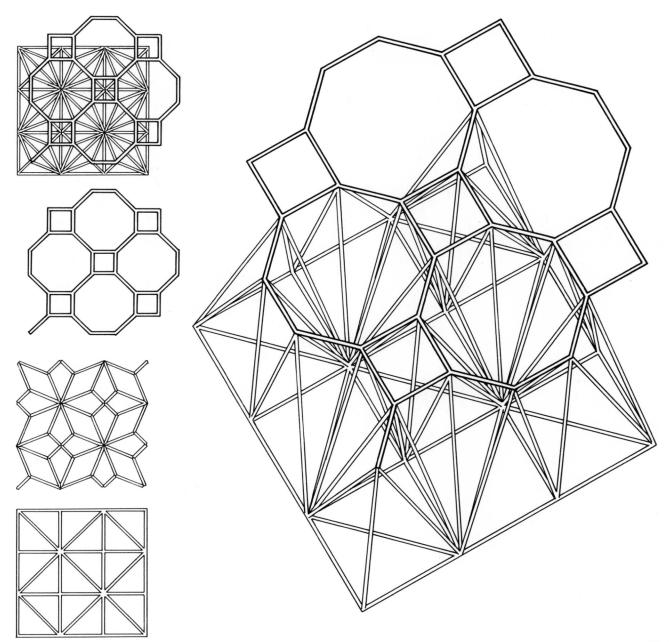

Plate 140
1. A skeletal space grid of right triangular-based pyramids. Interconnected apexes form a grid of alternating octagons and squares. *Component parts:* 2. Top grid formed by interconnected apexes. 3. Diagonal web members. 4. Bottom grid of right triangular-based pyramids. 5. Isometric of network.

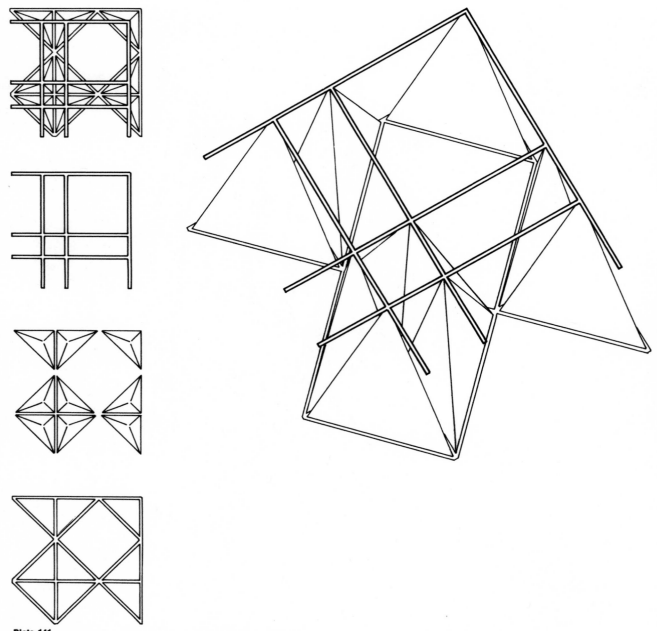

Plate 141
1. A stressed-skin space grid of right triangular-based pyramids with pyramids removed for lighter loads or internal openings. *Component parts:* 2. Top grid formed by interconnected apexes of pyramids.
3. Right triangular-based pyramids' edges and surfaces form the diagonal webbing. 4. Bottom grid formed by the interconnected bases of the pyramids. 5. Isometric of the network.

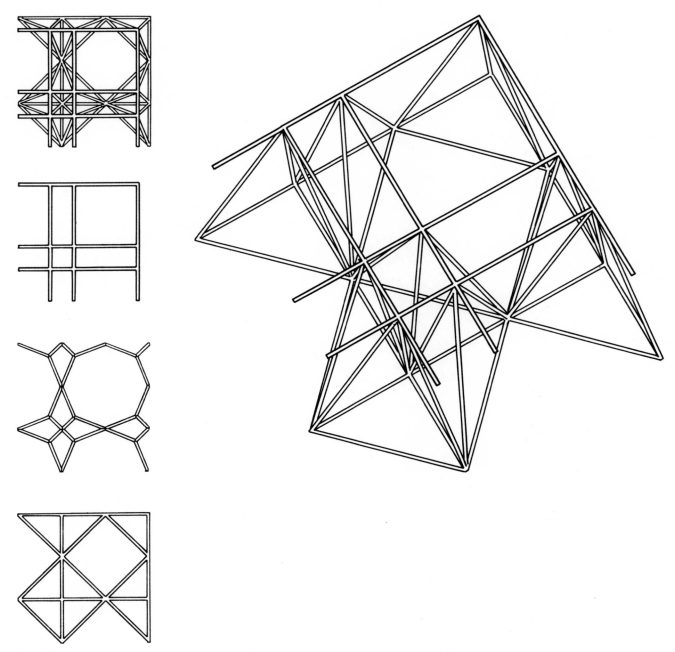

Plate 142
1. A skeletal space grid of right triangular-based pyramids with pyramids removed for lighter loading or internal openings. *Component parts:* 2. Top grid. 3. Diagonal web members. 4. Bottom grid. 5. Isometric of the network.

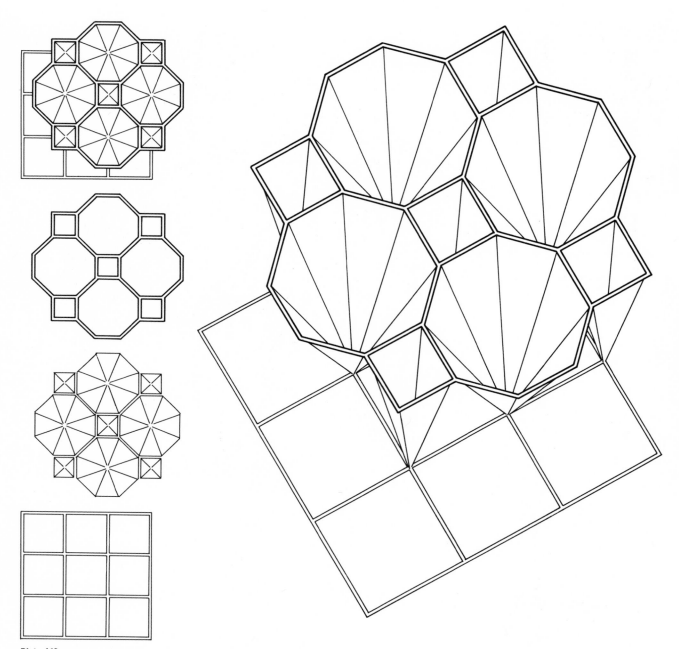

Plate 143
1. A stressed-skin space grid of alternating octagonal and square-based
pyramids whose interconnected apexes form an orthogonal grid.
Component parts: 2. Top grid formed by interconnected bases of
pyramids. 3. Octagonal and square-based pyramids' inclined edges
and surfaces provide the diagonal webbing. 4. Bottom grid formed by
interconnected apexes of pyramids. 5. Isometric of network.

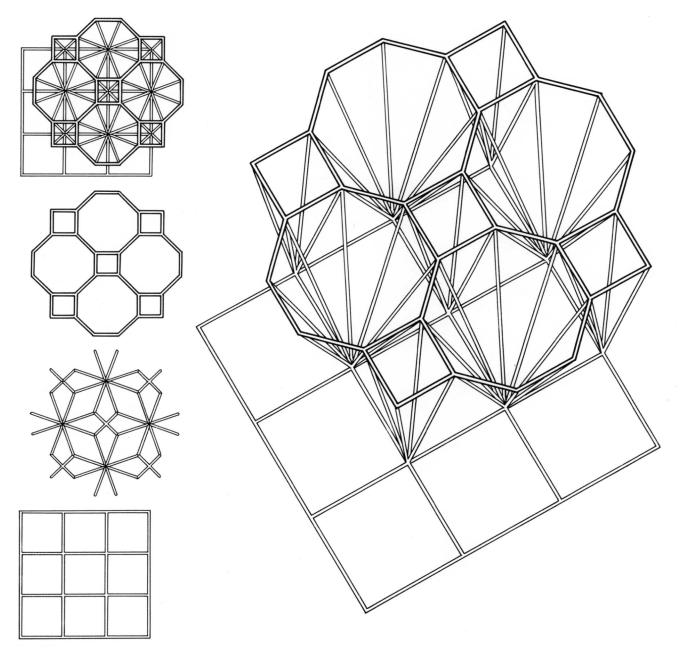

Plate 144
1. A skeletal space grid of alternating octagonal and square-based pyramids' interconnected apexes form an orthogonal grid. *Component parts:* 2. Top grid. 3. Diagonal web members. 4. Bottom grid. 5. Isometric of network.

Plate 145
1. A stressed-skin space grid of interconnected octagonal pyramids whose interconnected apexes form a diagonal grid. *Component parts:* 2. Top grid formed by interconnected bases of pyramids. 3. Octagonal pyramids' inclined edges and surfaces provide the diagonal webbing. 4. Bottom grid formed by interconnected pyramid apexes. 5. Isometric of network.

Plate 146
1. A skeletal space grid of octagonal-based pyramids whose interconnected apexes form an orthogonal grid. *Component parts:* 2. Top grid. 3. Diagonal web members. 4. Bottom grid. 5. Isometric of network.

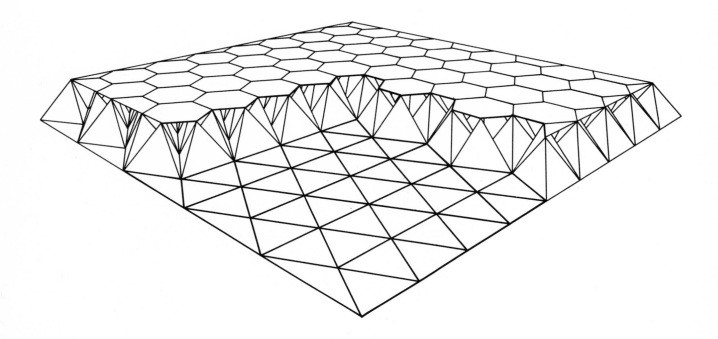

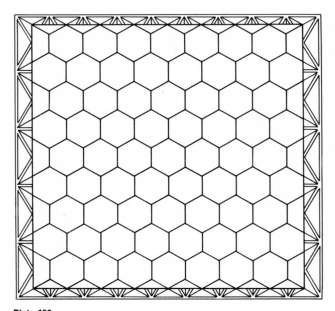

Plate 136
1. A skeletal space grid of right triangular-based pyramids. *Component parts:* 2. Top grid formed by right triangular-based tetrahedrons.
3. Diagonal web members. 4. Bottom grid. 5. Isometric of the network.

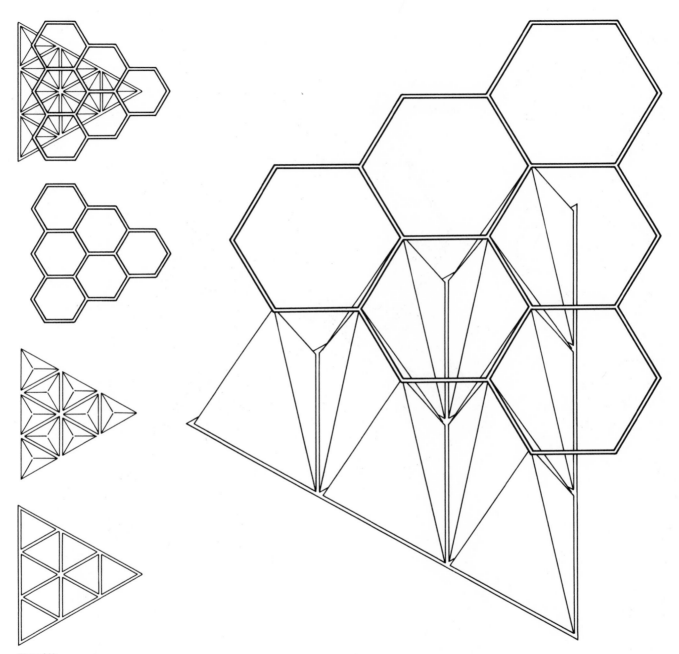

Plate 148
1. Stressed-skin space grid with tetrahedrons on a triangular grid.
Interconnected apexes form a hexagonal grid. *Component parts:*
2. Top grid formed by interconnected apexes of pyramids. 3. Pyramids'
inclined edges and surfaces provide diagonal webbing. 4. Bottom grid
formed by interconnected bases of pyramids. 5. Isometric of network.

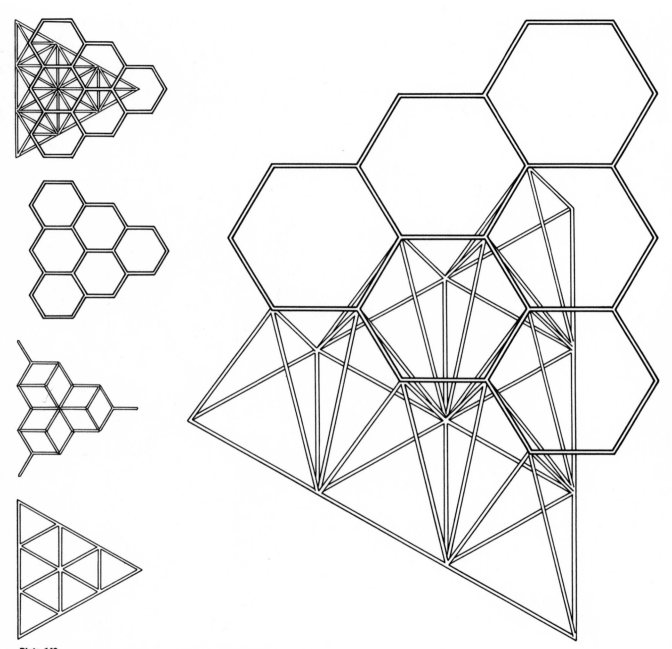

Plate 149
1. A skeletal space grid with a hexagonal top grid and a triangular bottom grid interconnected by diagonal web members. *Component parts:* 2. Top grid. 3. Diagonal web members. 4. Bottom grid. 5. Isometric of network.

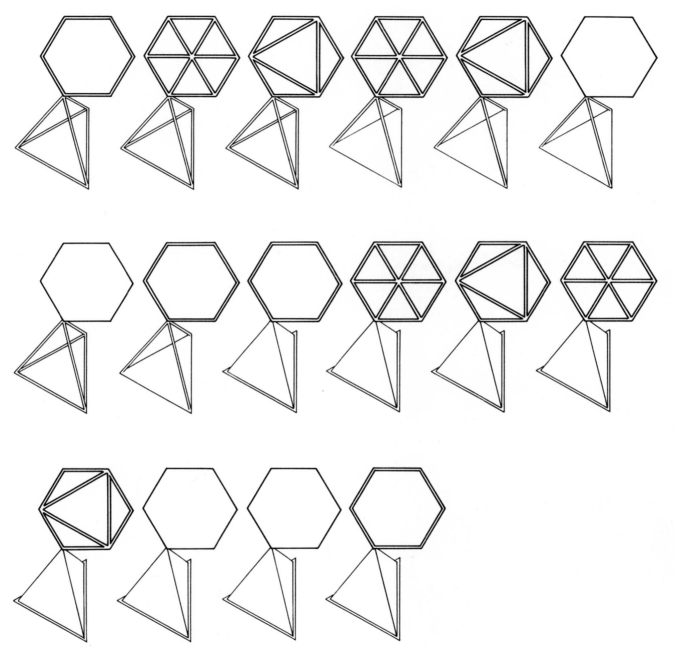

Plate 150
Combinations of members and surface used to stabilize the top and
bottom grid in various skeletal and stressed-skin space grids.

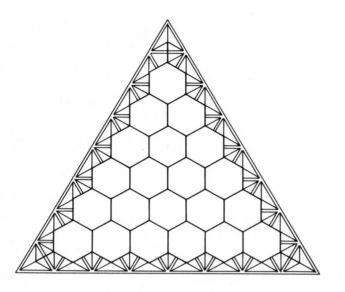

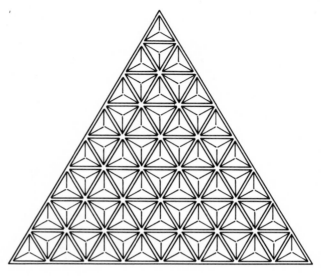

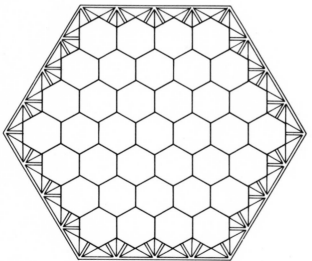

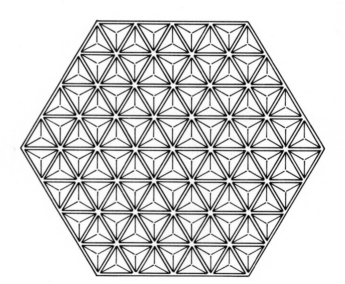

Plate 151
A stressed-skin space grid of tetrahedra on a triangular grid. Triangular periphery: 1. Top grid. 2. Bottom grid. Hexagonal periphery: 3. Top grid. 4. Bottom grid.

168

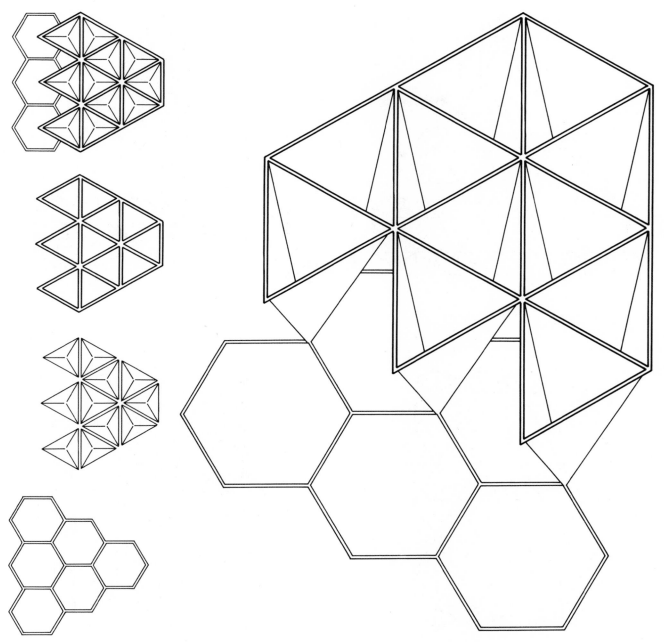

Plate 152
1. Triangular stressed-skin space grid with tetrahedrons on a triangular grid. The interconnected apexes form a hexagonal grid. *Component parts:* 2. Top grid. 3. Pyramids' inclined edges and surfaces provide the diagonal webbing. 4. Bottom grid. 5. Isometric of network.

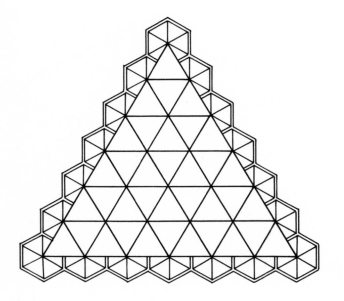
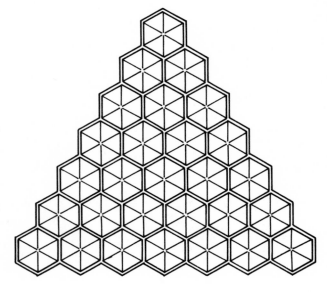
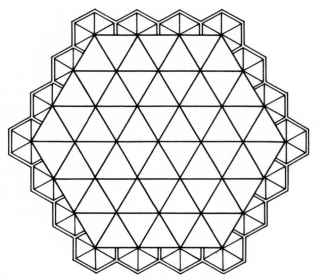
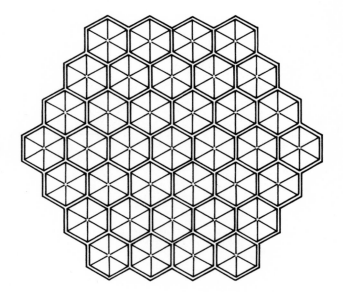

Plate 153
A stressed-skin space grid of hexagonal pyramids. Triangular periphery:
1. Top grid. 2. Bottom grid. Hexagonal periphery: 3. Top grid.
4. Bottom grid.

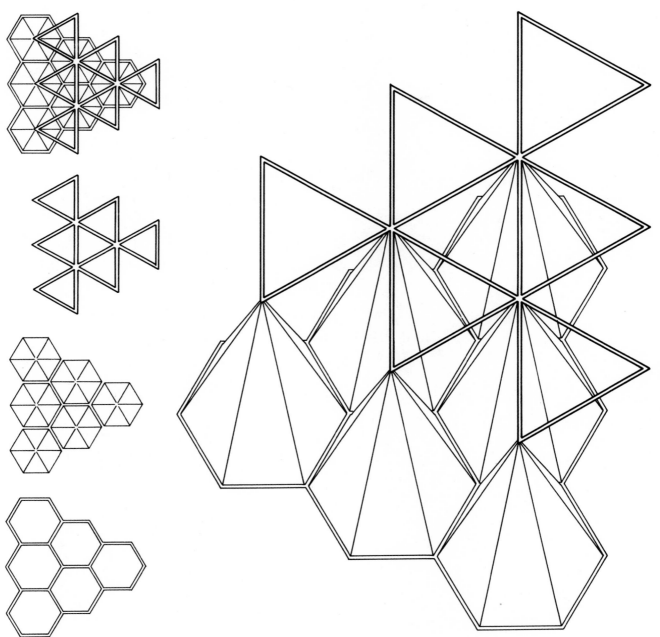

Plate 154
1. A stressed-skin space grid of hexagonal pyramids. *Component parts:*
2. Top grid is formed by the interconnected apexes of the pyramid.
3. Pyramids' inclined edges and surfaces provide the diagonal webbing.
4. Bottom grid formed by interconnected bases of hexagonal pyramids.
5. Isometric of network.

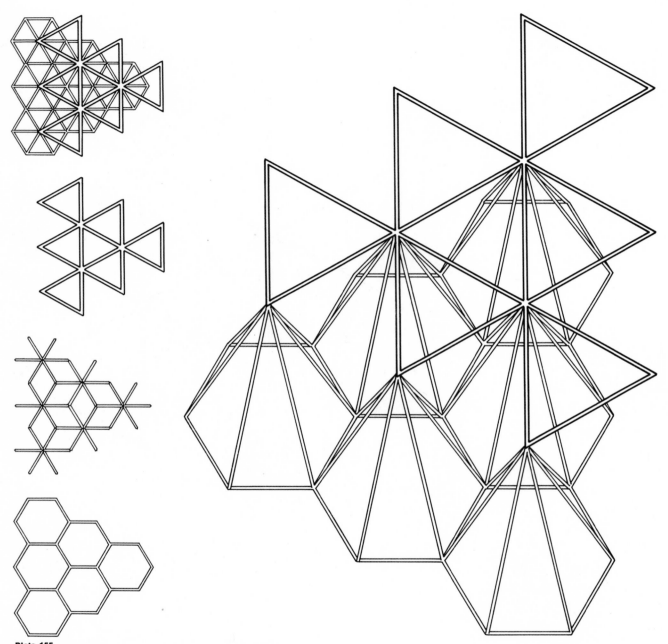

Plate 155
1. A skeletal space grid of a triangular top grid and a hexagonal bottom grid, interconnected by diagonal web members. *Component parts:* 2. Top grid. 3. Diagonal web members. 4. Bottom grid. 5. Isometric of network.

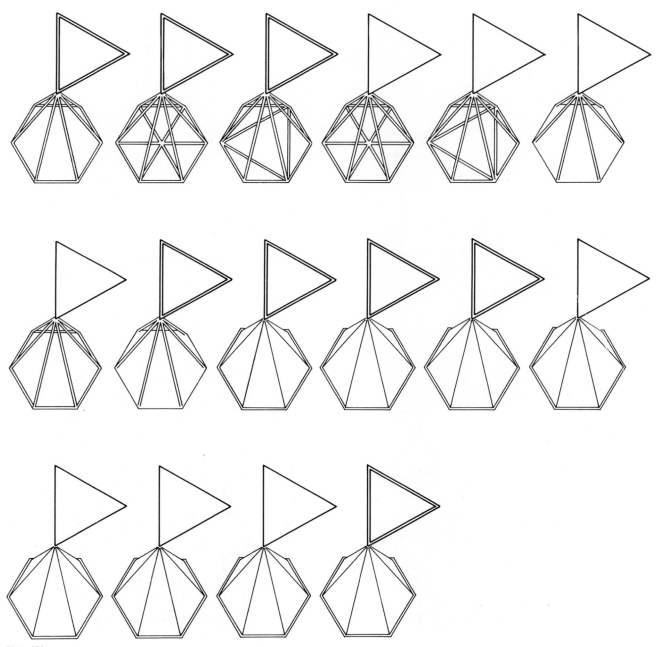

Plate 156
Combinations of members and surfaces used to stabilize the top and bottom grids of various triangular or hexagonal skeletal or stressed-skin space grids.

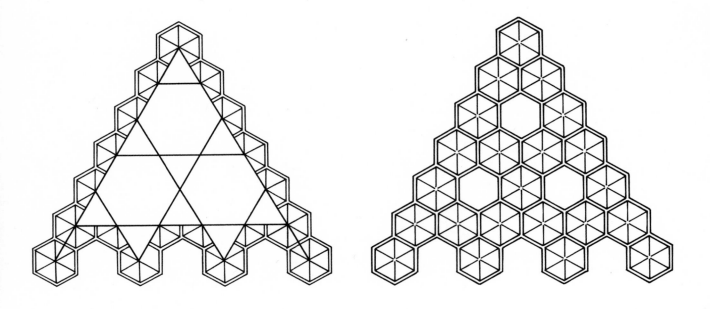

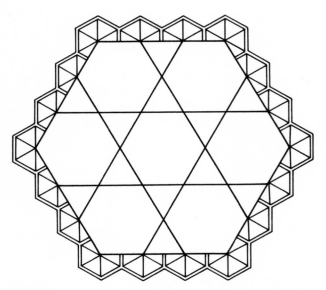

Plate 157
A stressed-skin space grid of hexagonal pyramids eliminating pyramids
for lighter loading or internal openings. Triangular periphery: 1. Top
grid. 2. Bottom grid. Hexagonal periphery: 3. Top grid. 4. Bottom grid.

174

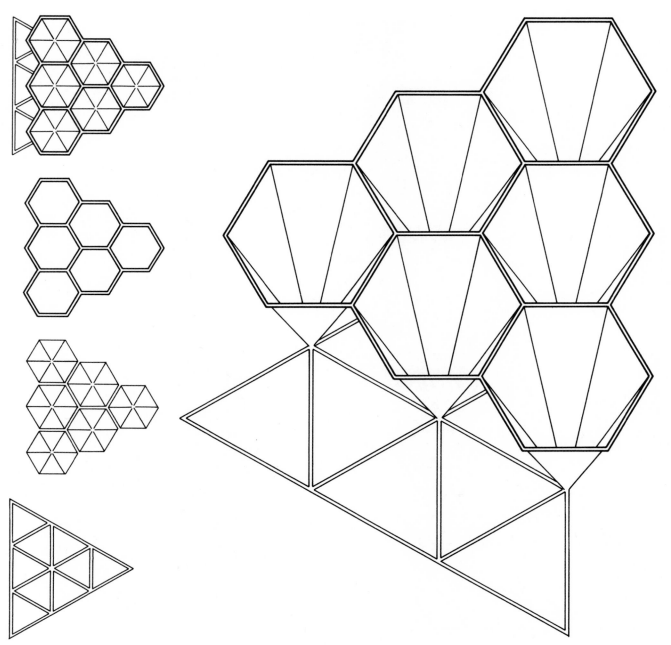

Plate 158

1. A stressed-skin space grid of hexagonal pyramids whose interconnected apexes form a triangular grid. *Component parts:* 2. Top grid. 3. Pyramids' inclined edges and surfaces provide diagonal webbing. 4. Bottom grid. 5. Isometric of network.

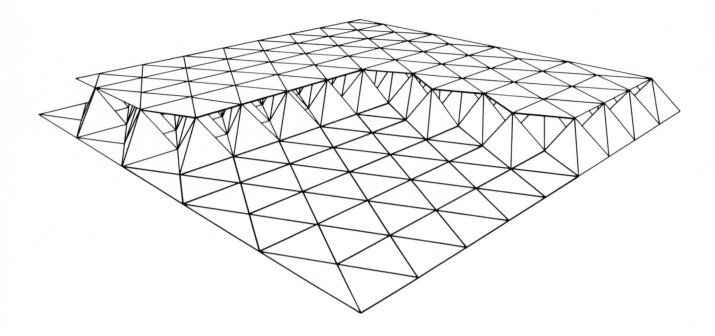

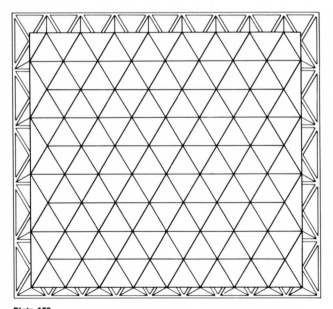

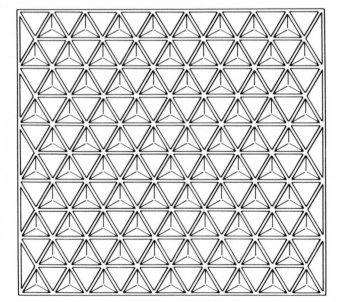

Plate 159
1. Perspective of a stressed-skin space grid of tetrahedrons on a triangular grid with pyramids removed. 2. Top grid. 3. Bottom grid.

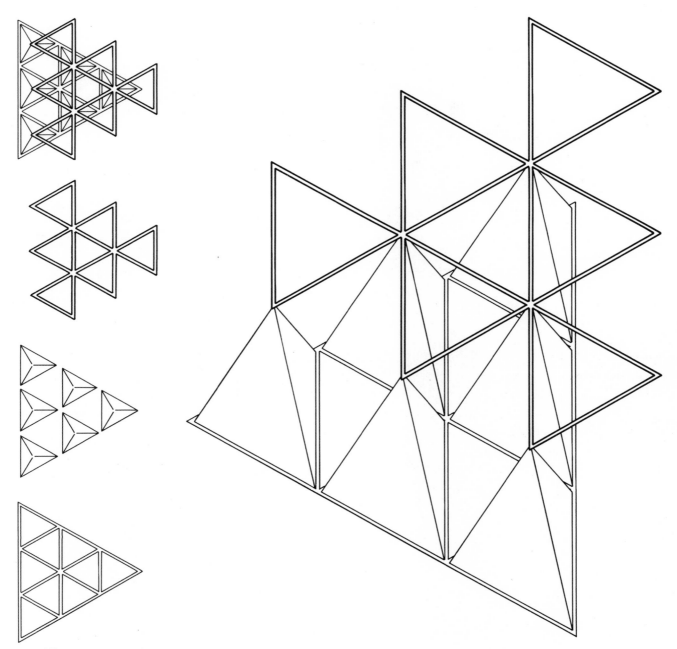

Plate 160
1. A stressed-skin space grid of tetrahedrons on a triangular grid. Interconnected apexes form a triangular grid. This system is the most stable. *Component parts:* 2. Top grid formed by interconnected apexes of pyramids. 3. Pyramids' inclined edges and surfaces provide diagonal webbing. 4. Bottom grid formed by interconnected bases of pyramids. 5. Isometric of network.

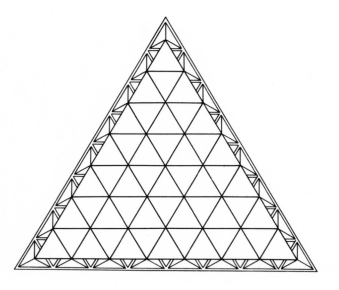

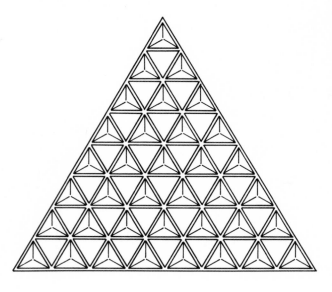

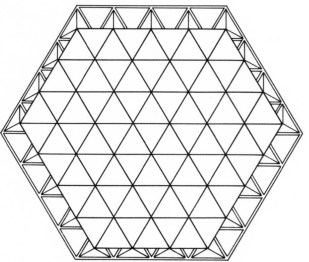

Plate 161
A stressed-skin space grid of tetrahedrons on a triangular grid with pyramids removed. Triangular periphery: 1. Top grid. 2. Bottom grid. Hexagonal periphery; 3. Top grid. 4. Bottom grid.

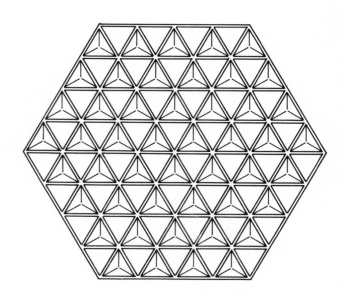

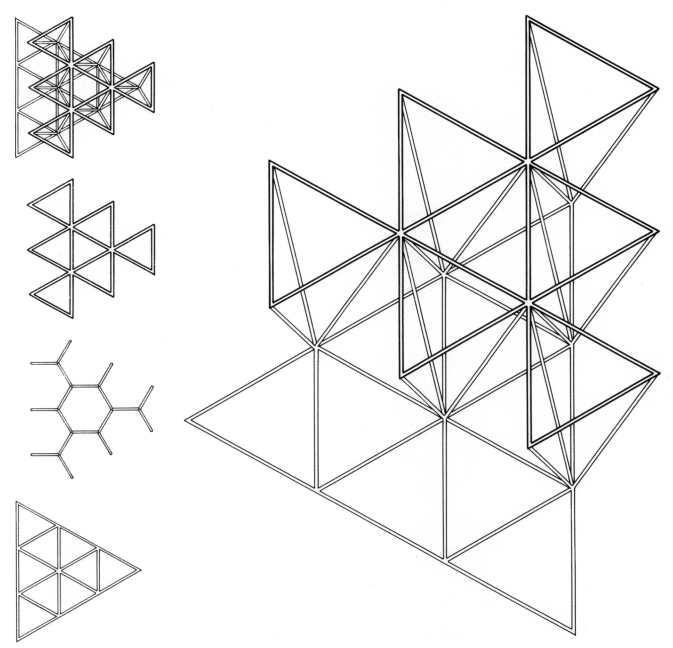

Plate 162
1. A skeletal space grid with top and bottom triangular grids
interconnected by diagonal web members, formed by alternating
octahedrons and tetrahedrons. *Component parts:* 2. Top grid. 3. Diagonal
web members. 4. Bottom grid. 5. Isometric of network.

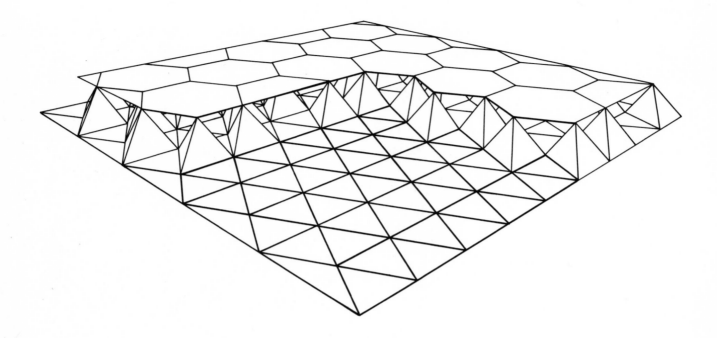

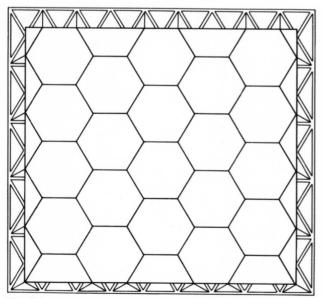

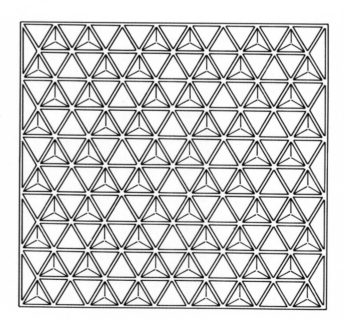

Plate 163
1. A perspective of a stressed-skin space grid with internal pyramid removed for lighter loading or internal openings. 2. Top grid hexagonal.
3. Bottom grid triangular.

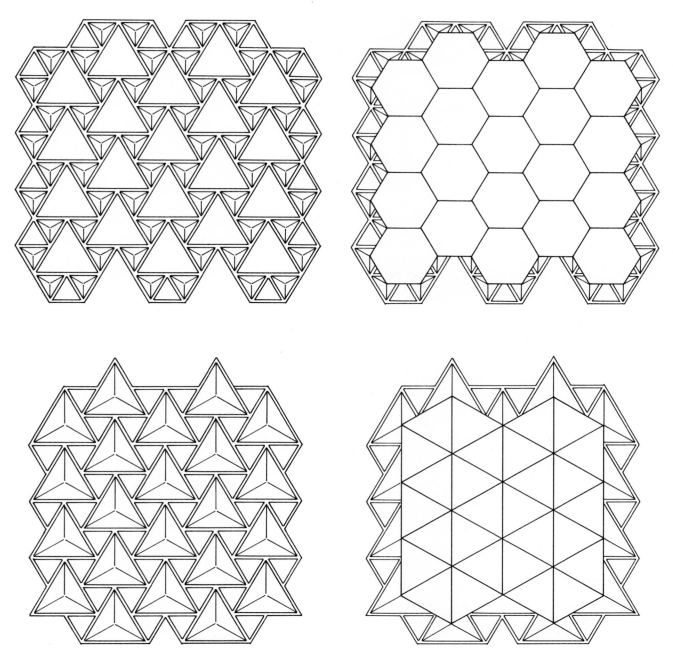

Plate 164
Triangular stressed-skin space grids with triangular internal openings.
Internal pyramids are removed for lighter loads or internal openings.
1. Top grid. 2. Bottom grid. 3. Top grid. 4. Bottom grid.

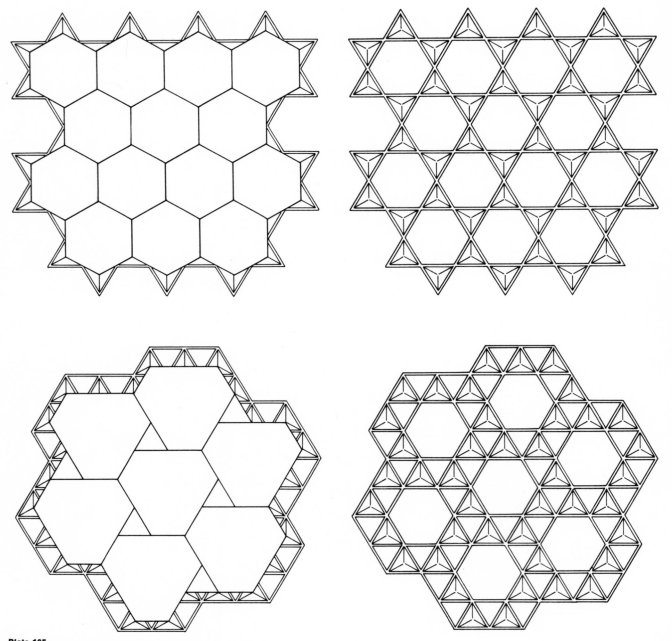

Plate 165
Triangular stressed-skin space grids with hexagonal internal openings.
1. Top grid. 2. Bottom grid. 3. Top grid. 4. Bottom grid.

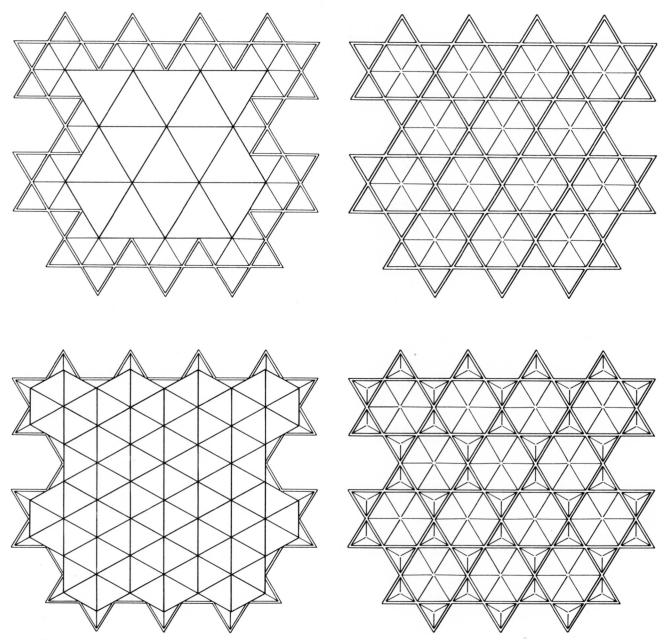

Plate 166
Triangular grid with hexagonal pyramids. 1. Top grid. 2. Bottom grid.
Triangular pyramids. 1. Top grid. 2. Bottom grid.

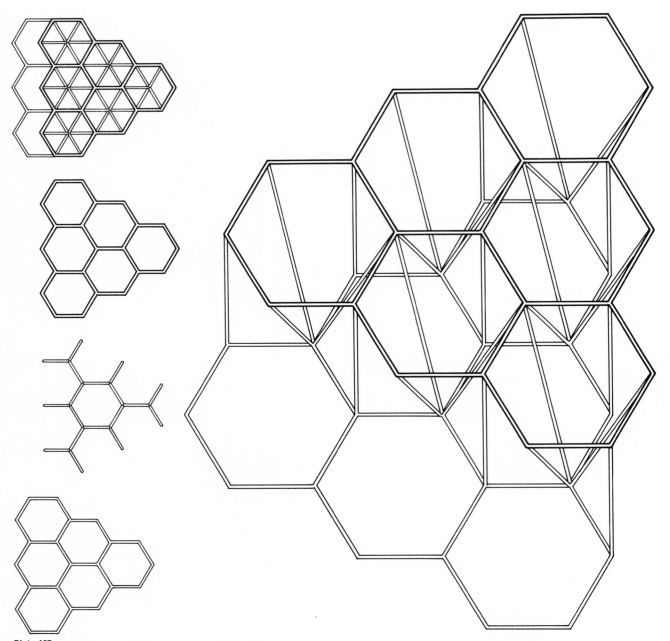

Plate 167
1. A skeletal space grid with hexagonal top and bottom grids.
Component parts: 2. Top grid. 3. Diagonal and vertical web members.
4. Bottom grid. 5. Isometric of network.

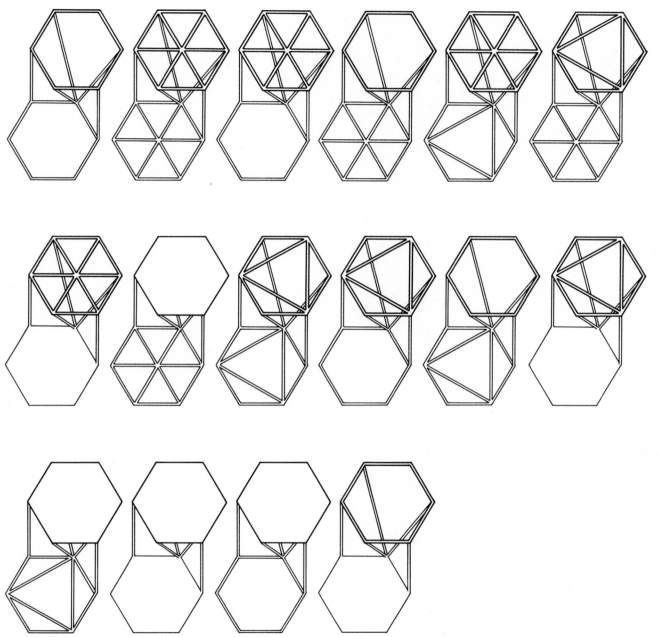

Plate 168
Combinations of members and surfaces used to stabilize top and bottom grids.

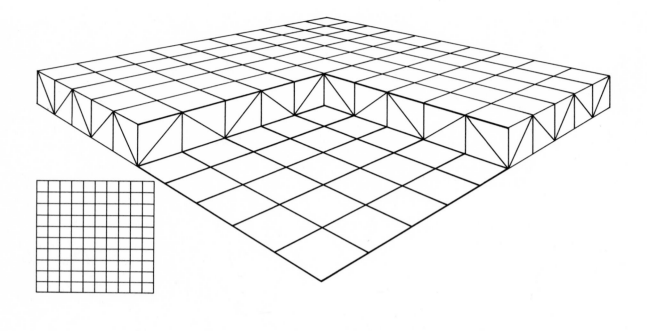

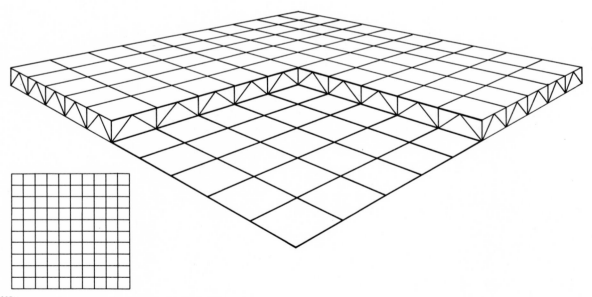

Plate 169
Lattice space grids of intersecting vertical trusses forming an orthogonal
network.

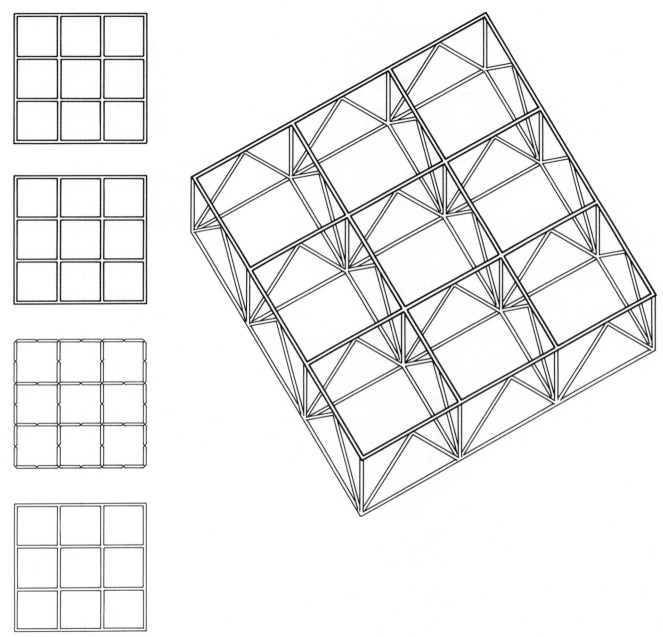

Plate 170

1. A lattice space grid of intersecting vertical trusses forming an orthogonal network. *Component parts:* 2. Top grid. 3. Diagonal and vertical web members. 4. Bottom grid. 5. Isometric of network.

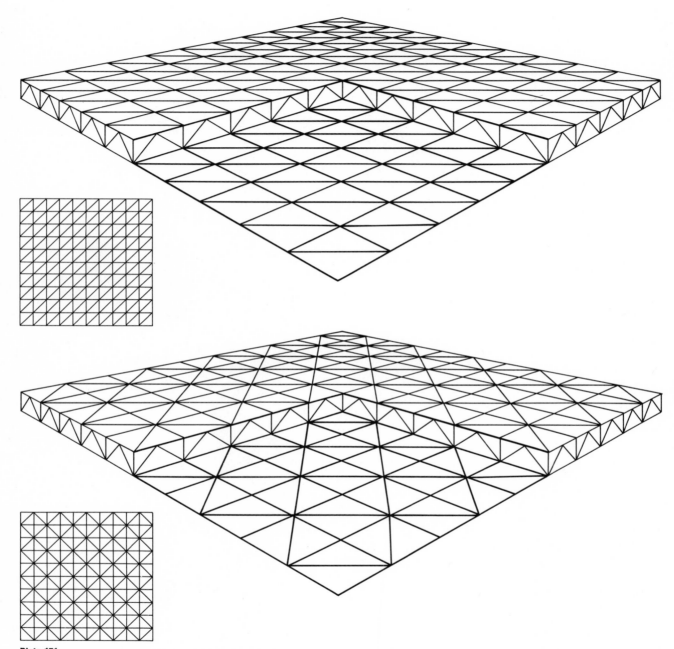

Plate 171
Lattice space grids of intersecting vertical trusses forming a right
triangular network.

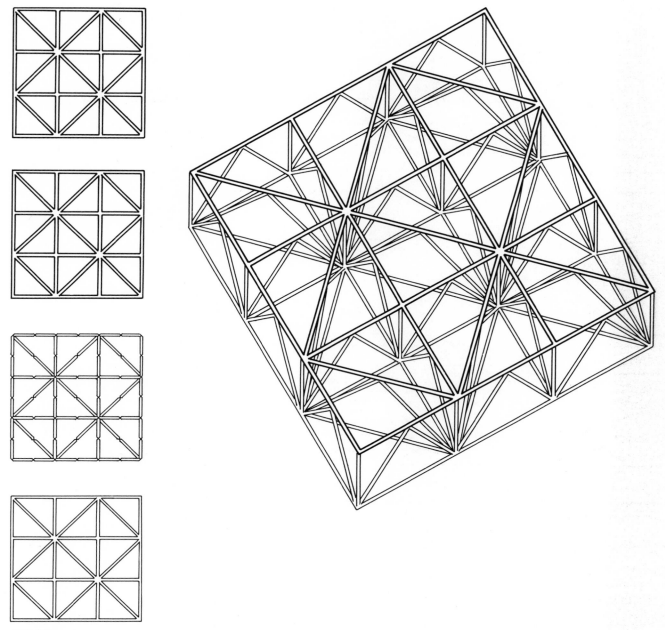

Plate 172
1. A lattice space grid of trusses forming a right triangular grid.
Component parts: 2. Top grid. 3. Diagonal and vertical web members.
4. Bottom grid. 5. Isometric of network.

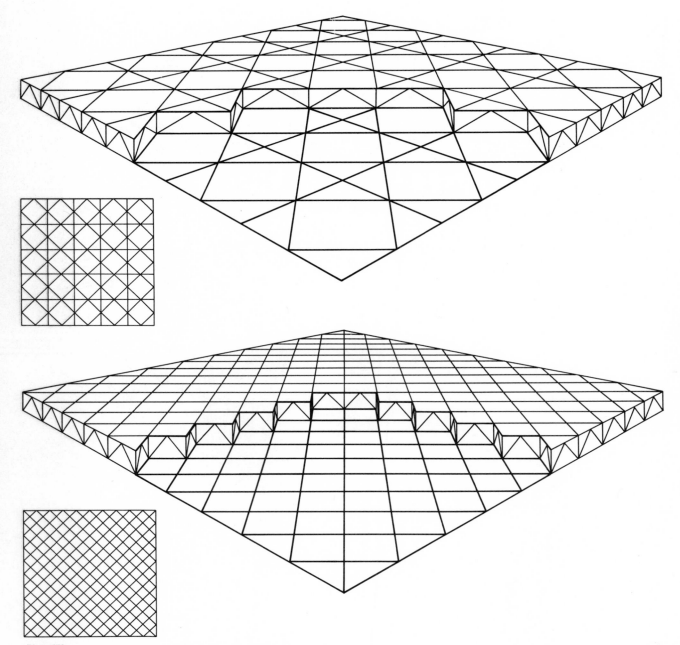

Plate 173
1. A lattice space grid of intersecting vertical trusses forming a grid
of alternating squares and right triangles, a combination of the
diagonal and orthogonal networks.

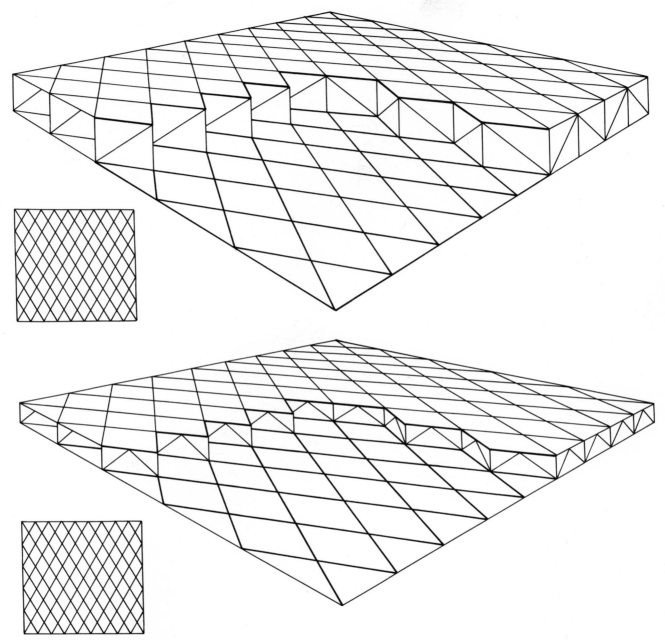

Plate 174
Lattice space grids of intersecting vertical trusses forming a skewed
network.

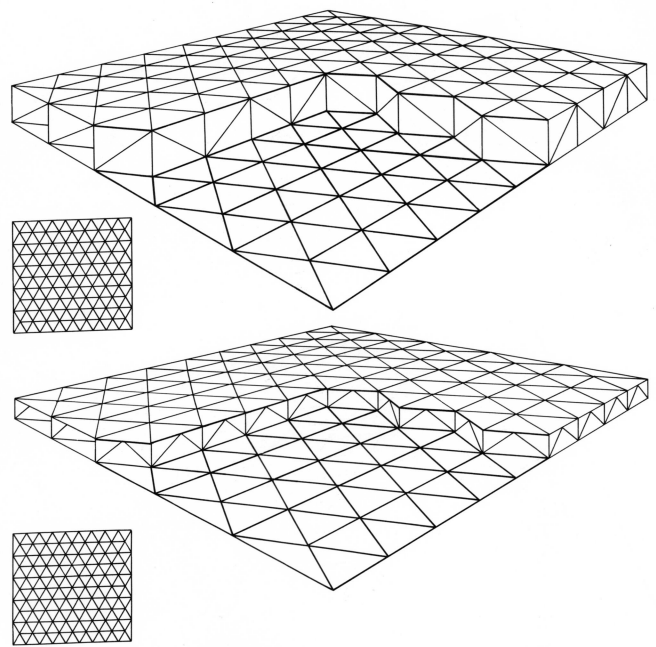

Plate 175
A lattice space grid of intersecting vertical trusses forming a triangular
network.

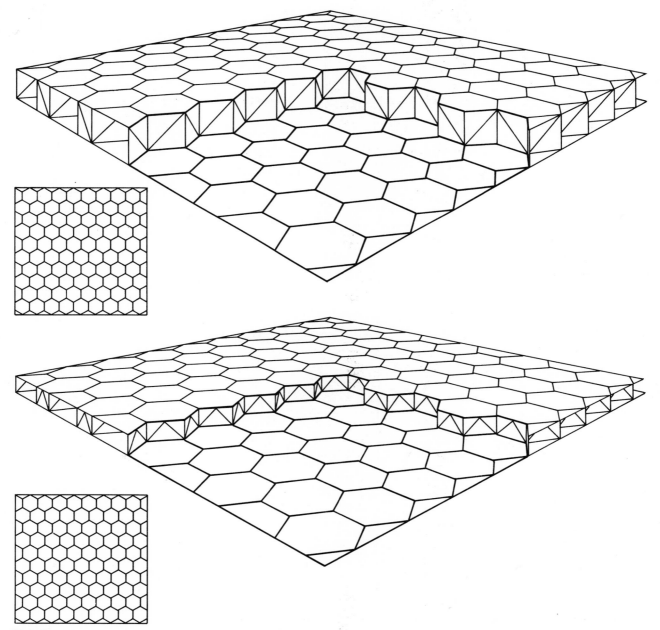

Plate 176
A lattice space grid of intersecting vertical trusses forming a hexagonal
network.

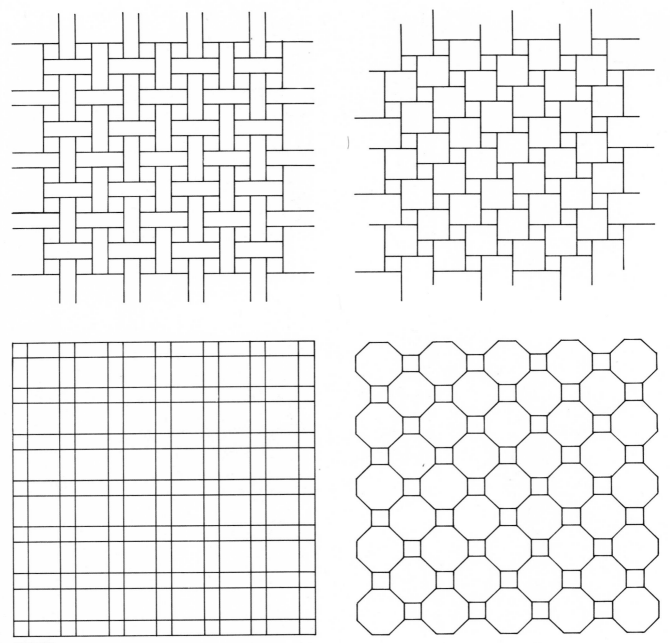

Plate 178
Lattice space grids of intersecting vertical trusses, combinations of triangular and hexagonal prisms.

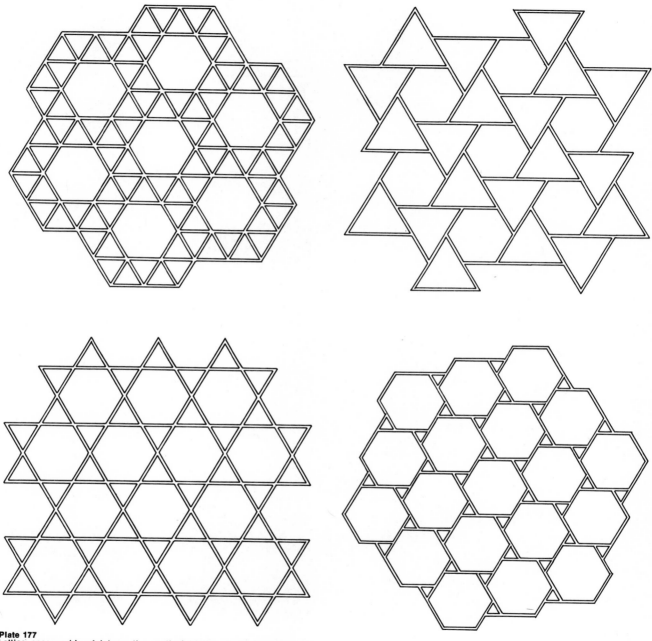

Plate 177
Lattice space grids of intersecting vertical trusses. 1.–3. Orthogonal network with internal openings. 4. Network of octagonal and square prisms.

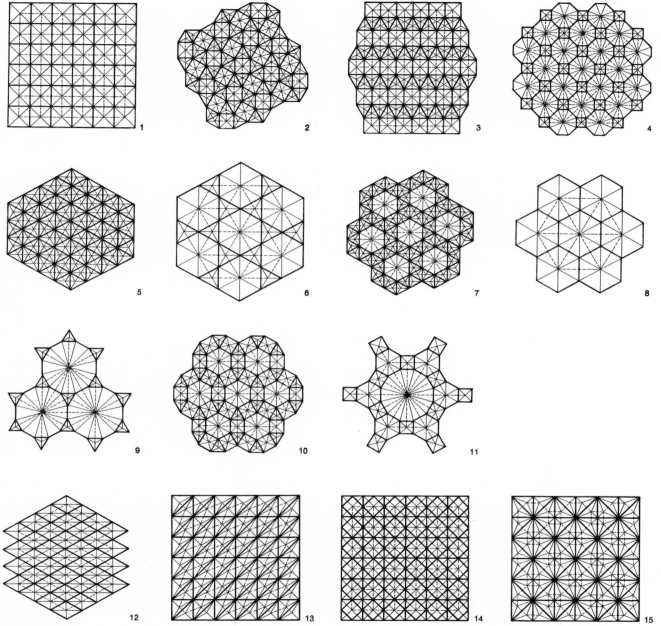

Plate 180
Differential and offset, two- three- and four-way double-layer space grids, formed from regular and semiregular polygons and other triangulated grids. 1. square, 2. right-hand triangle-square, 3. alternating triangle-square, 4. octagon-square, 5. triangle, 6. lesser triangle-hexagon 7. right-hand greater triangle-hexagon, 10. hexagon, 11. triangle dodecagon, 10. triangle-square-hexagon, 11. square-hexagon-dodecagon, 12. skewed, 13. diagonally braced square, 14. braced square, 15. diagonally braced square. Two-way systems: 1, 2, 3, 4, 12. Three-way systems: 5, 6, 7, 8, 9, 10, 11, 13. Four-way systems: 14, 15. The only offset is 12, skewed.

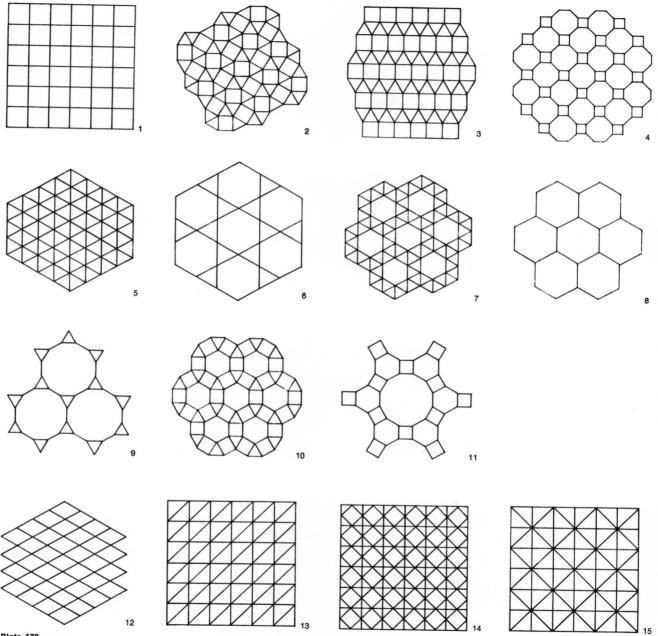

Plate 179
Lattice and direct two-, three-, and four-way double-layer space grids, formed from regular and semiregular polygons and other triangulated grids. 1. square, 2. right-hand triangle-square, 3. alternating triangle-square, 4. octagon-square, 5. triangle, 6. lesser triangle-hexagon, 7. right-hand greater triangle-hexagon, 8. hexagon, 9. triangle dodecagon, 10. triangle-square-hexagon, 11. square-hexagon-dodecagon, 12. skewed, 13. diagonally braced square, 14. square, braced. 15. diagonally braced square. Two-way systems: 1, 2, 3, 4, 12, 15. Three-way systems: 5, 6, 7, 10, 11, 13. Four-way systems: 14, 15.

Aggour, M. S. "Space frame action and load distribution In Skew Bridges." I.A.B.S.E., 5 Congress, Rio de Janeiro, 1964, Prelim. Publ., p. 647.

Bond D. "Design, model analysis and testing of a 83 ft. span interconnected portal grillage." *The Structural Engineer*, April 1963, pp. 127–133.

Booth, L. G. and B. T. Keay "The Functional and Structural Requirements of Timber Space Frames as Industrialized Components," Paper No. L2; International Conference on Space Structures, London, 1966.

Brown, A. J. and W. Tengi. "Raising the roof at Air Force Academy." *Steel Construction Digest*, Vol. 15, No. 1, 1958.

Brown, P., H. Ferrera, A. Gonzales, J. Jerde, R. Kraft, R. Smith. "A longspan structure with minimum support having maximum usable space within and below the structures for an undefined function." B.A. Thesis, University of Southern California, Los Angeles, Calif., 1965.

Burns, R. "Precast floor system." M.Arch. Thesis, School of Architecture and Planning, Massachusetts Institute of Technology, Cambridge, Mass., 1962.

du Chateau, S. "Hanging roofs, metallic shell roofs, and lattice roofs: the SDC structural system." (Colloqium), Proceedings of the International Association of Shell Structures at Paris, in 1962. North Holland Publishing Co., Amsterdam, 1963, pp. 288–300.

du Chateau, S. "Nouvelles structures tubulaires." *L'architecture d'aujourd'hui*, No. 75, 1958.

du Chateau, S. "Structure spatiale spherique en trame tridirectionelle." *L'architecture d'aujourd'hui*, No. 81, 1959.

Coy, P. H. "Structural analysis of Unistrut space frame roofs." University of Michigan Press, Ann Arbor, Michigan, 1955.

Critchow, K. "Universal space families." *Architectural Design*, October 1965, pp. 514–517.

Curtis, J. W. "Technology and the architect." *Architecture and Building*, March 1958, p. 82.

Davies, D. K. "Laboratory research center," M.Arch. Thesis, School of Architecture and Planning, Massachusetts Institute of Technology, Cambridge, Mass., 1965.

Diamant, R. M. E. *Industrialized Building* 2 (Second Series). Iliffe Books Ltd., London, 1965.

Dodds, S. "The work of Jeffrey Lindsay." *Canadian Architect*, Toronto, Canada, Vol. 2, No. 3, March 1957, pp. 18–26.

Doernach, R. "Spharische Raumfachwerke." *Der Stahlbau*, April 1960, pp. 97–104.

English, J. M. "Optimization of framing arrangements for large metal roof systems." Publications IABSE, Vol. 20, 1960, p. 75.

Enneper, P. "Der Krupp-Pavillon auf der Messe in Hannover," *Acier, Stahl, Steel*, vol. 22, February 1957, pp. 71–78.

Ewell, W. W. "Three-dimensional displacement diagram for space frame structures." Proc. A.S.C.E., May 1950.

Ewell, W. W., Sokubo and J. I. Abrams. "Deflection in gridworks and slabs." Trans. A.S.C.E., Vol. 117, 1952, pp. 869–912.

Fader, J. "Grid analysis by the reaction distribution method." Journal of the Structural Division, Proc. A.S.C.E., August 1961, pp. 77–103.

Federhofer, K. "Graphische Kinematik und Kineostatik des starren räumlichen Systems." ZAMM 9 (1929), Heft 4, pp. 312–318.

Fortey, J. W. and N. W. Krahl. "Stress analysis of space frames." *Civil Engineering*, February 1961, pp. 60–61.

Friedman. "Urbanism Mobile." *l'architecture d'aujourd'hui*, No. 102, June–July 1962.

Fröhlich, J. "Oktaplatte in Rohrkonstruktion." *Der Stahlbau*, 28 Jahrg. St. 255/256. Heft 9. Sept. 1959.

Fuller, R. Buckminster. "Industrial Logistics and Design Strategy." The Pennsylvania Triangle, 1952.

Gilkie, Ronald C. "A Comparison between the theoretical and experimental analysis of a stressed-skin structure in plastics and aluminum." Paper No. K2, International Conference on Space Structures, London 1966.

Hall, A. S. and R. W. Woodhead. *Frame Analysis.* John Wiley & Sons, New York, 1961.

Hamilton, W. and G. P. Manning. "Aluminum dome structures and long span roof units." *Civil Engineering*, Vol. 13, No. 5, May 1959, pp. 263–266.

Hamilton, W. and G. P. Manning. "Some structural uses of aluminum alloy with special reference to domes." *Journal, Institution of Structural Engineers*, vol. 31, No. 12, Dec. 1953, pp. 337–350.

Hilbert, D. and S. Cohn-Vossen. *Geometry and the Imagination.* Chelsea Publishing Co., New York, 1952.

"Jointitis." *Architectural Forum*, August–September, 1964, pp. 94–97.

Kahn, Louis. "Philadelphia City Hall." *L'architecture d'aujourd'hui*, No. 105, Dec. Jan. 1963.

Kato, T. and K. Takanashi. "Die Spannungsanalysis und der versuch von der Oktaplatte." Proceedings of the symposium on the new ideas in structural design, Japan Society for the Promotion of Science, Tokyo, 1963. pp. 41–48.

Ketoff, S. "Les structures tridimensionnelles et leurs possibilités d'application." *L'architecture d'aujourd'hui*, No. 99. Dec. 1961.

Kupritz, P. "Precast floor systems." M.Arch Thesis, Massachusetts Institute of Technology, 1962.

Layton, T. "Prototype structure for a research and development building." M.Arch Thesis, Massachusetts Institute of Technology, 1965.

Li, Shu-t'ien. "Matrix analysis of indeterminate space trusses." Publications, I.A.B.S.E., Zurich, Switzerland, Vol. 22, 1962, pp. 129–143.

Lindsay, J. "Space Frames and Structural Physics." *Arts and Architecture*, July 1957.

Lindgreen. *Geometric Dissections.* D. Van Nostrand Co. Inc. Princeton, New Jersey, 1964.

Livesley, R. K. "The application of an electronic digital computer to some problems of structural analysis." *Structural Engineer*, January 1956, pp. 1–12.

Livesley, R. K. "Matrix methods of structural analysis." Pergamon Press, Inc., New York, 1964.

Lozar, C. "Prototype structure for a research and development building." M.Arch., Thesis, Massachusetts Institute of Technology, 1965.

MacMahon, P. A. *New Mathematical Pastimes.* University Press, Cambridge, Mass.

Makowski, Z. S., and A. J. S. Pippard. "Experimental analysis of space structures, with particular reference to braced domes." Proc. I.C.E., Part III, Dec. 1952, pp. 420–441.

Makowski, Z. S. "Interconnected systems, two and three-dimensional grids." *The Guilds' Engineer*, 1955, pp. 11–28.

Makowski, Z. S. "Influence of the torsional rigidity upon the stress distribution in grid frameworks analyzed by the orthotropic plate analogy." *Biuletyn Inzyniery-jno-Budowlany*, Institution of Polish Engineers in Great Britain. September 1956, series 11/5, pp. 78–92.

Makowski, Z. S. "An analysis of open grid framework." *Civil and Structural Engineers Review.* July 1957, pp. 341–347.

Makowski, Z. S. and R. Ramirez. "Modern grid frameworks of a regular hexagonal layout." *Technika i Nauka, Journal of the Institution of Polish Engineers abroad,* No. 5, 1959, pp. 1–41.

Makowski, Z. S. and R. Ramirez. "Plastics as components in dome and roof structures." *Transactions and Journal of the Plastics Institute,* No. 73, February 1960, pp. 26–29.

Makowski, Z. S. "Modern grid structures." *Architectural Science Review,* Vol. 3, No. 2, July 1960, pp. 52–65.

Makowski, Z. S. "Double-layer grid structures." *Architectural Association Journal,* March 1961, pp. 218–238.

Makowski, Z. S. "Developments in aluminum sheet space structures." *Light Metals,* Vol. 24, No. 275, April 1961, pp. 110–113.

Makowski, Z. S. "Space structures—modern trends and recent developments." published by the School of Architecture, The Polytechnic, London, 1961.

Makowski, Z. S. "Stressed skin space grids." *Architectural Design,* July 1961, pp. 323–327.

Makowski, Z. S. "Aluminum sheet structures." *Light Metals,* July 1961.

Makowski, Z. S., and P. Mukhopadhyay. "Analytical and experimental stress analysis of double-layer grid frameworks." *Technika i Nauka,* No. 13, December 1961, pp. 43–68.

Makowski, Z. S. "Structures spatiales—théorie et applications." *L'architecture d'aujourd'hui,* No. 99, January 1962. pp. 78–80.

Makowski, Z. S. "Recent developments in stressed sheet space systems." *Tekkoto-Kinsoku Sha,* No. 2. (in English and Japanese) March 1962, pp. 17–23.

Makowski, Z. S. "Sheet space systems." *The Guild's Engineer,* 1962.

Makowski, Z. S. "Space structures in steel." *Building with Steel: Journal of the British Constructional Steelwork Association,* Vol. 11, No. 4, November 1962, pp. 4–7.

Makowski, Z. S. "Recent trends and developments in three-dimensional frameworks." *Civil Engineering and Public Works Review,* Vol. 57, No. 676, November 1962, pp. 1441–1443. Vol. 57, No. 677, December 1962, pp. 1561–1564.

Makowski, Z. S. "Structural use of plastics in stressed skin construction." *Applied Plastics,* Vol. 6, No. 2, February 1963, pp. 47–52.

Makowski, Z. S. "Space structures in plastic." *Plastics,* Vol. 28, No. 304, February 1963. Vol. 28, No. 305, March 1963, pp. 66–67.

Makowski, Z. S. "Modern architecture and space structures." (In Italian) Published by the University of Naples, Faculty of Engineering, Napoli, 1962. Istituto di Architettura e Composizione Architettonica, Seminario di Studi-Architettura.

Makowski, Z. S. "Space structures" (In English and Japanese). Column No. 5, January 1963, pp. 21–58. Published by Yawata Iron & Steel Co. Ltd. Tokyo.

Makowski, Z. S. "The structural use of plastics in building." *Plastics in Building,* second edition 1963, pp. 47–53.

Makowski, Z. S. "Wider range of structural uses of plastics." *The Financial Times,* June 1963, p. 6.

Makowski, Z. S. *Räumliche Tragwerke aus Stahl.* Published by Verlag Stahleisen, Dusseldorf, 1963.

Makowski, Z. S. "Recent developments in stressed-sheet space grid systems." Proceedings of the World Conference on Shell Structures, San Francisco, 1963.

Makowski, Z. S. "Aluminum space structures." Symposium of Aluminum in Structural Engineering. London, June 11 and 12, 1963.

Makowski, Z. S. "Aluminum space structures." Proceedings of the symposium on aluminum in Structural Engineering, June 1964, London, pp. 195–207 and 313–315. Published by the Institution of Structural Engineers and Aluminum Federation.

Makowski, Z. S. "Modern trends and recent developments of light-weight structures." Column No. 9, January 1964, pp. 69–90. Published in English and Japanese by Tekko-to-Kinzoku Co. Tokyo, Japan.

Makowski, Z. S. "Growing use of plastics." *The Financial Times,* June 22, 1964, inset on industrialized building, p. 6.

Makowski, Z. S. "A review of plastics structures around the world." *Plastics in Building,* August 1964, pp. 5–9.

Makowski, Z. S. "Constructions spatiales en acier." Published by Centre belgo-luxembourgeois d'information de L'Acier, Brussels, 1964.

Makowski, Z. S. "Plastic structures." *Building Materials,* October 1964, pp. 24–27.

Makowski, Z. S. "The structural applications of plastics." *The Architect and Building News,* November 4, 1964, pp. 889–892.

Makowski, Z. S. "Use of prefabricated steel space frames." *Civil Engineering, A Financial Times Survey,* November 16, 1964, pp. 28–29.

Makowski, Z. S. "Research on structural applications of plastics." *Interbuild,* November 1964, pp. 16–25.

Makowski, Z. S. "Plastics to carry weight." *Spectrum,* May 1965, pp. 6–7.

Makowski, Z. S. and B. S. Benjamin. "The analysis of folded-plate structures in plastics." Conference on Plastics in Building Structures, June, 1965.

Makowski, Z. S. "Applicazioni strutturali delle materie plastiche." *Materie Plastiche e Elastomeri,* No. 6, June 1965, pp. 622–633.

Makowski, Z. S. "Raumtragwerke." *Bauwelt,* No. 29/30, Berlin. July 26, 1965, pp. 809–825.

Makowski, Z. S. "Analytical and experimental investigations of stress distribution in steel space frames." Proceedings of the Steel Congress 1964, Progress in Steel Construction Work, pp. 581–606, published in 1965 by the High Authority of the European Coal & Steel Community, Luxembourg.

Makowski, Z. S. "Estructuras espaciales de plásticos." *Revista del instituto para el desarrollo de los materiales plásticos en la construcción,* Buenos Aires.

Makowski, Z. S. *Steel space structures.* Michael Joseph Ltd., London, 1965.

Makowski, Z. S. "The structural applications of plastics." *Plastics in Building Construction,* pp. 49–78, Blackie & Sons Ltd. 1965.

Makowski, Z. S. "Developments in aluminum sheet space structures." *Light Metals,* April 1961.

Makowski, Z. S. "Plastics as components in dome and roof structures." Trans. The Plastics Institute, Vol. 28, No. 73, February 1960.

Makowski, Z. S. "Constructions spatiales en acier." Centre belgo-luxembourgeois d'information de L'Acier, Brussels, 1964.

Makowski, Z. S. *Steel space structures. A comprehensive review.* Michael Joseph Ltd., 26 Bloomsbury St., London, W.C.I.

Makowski, Z. S. "Use of prefabricated steel space frames." *Civil Engineering, A Financial Times Survey,* November 16, 1964, pp. 28–29.

Martin, J. and J. Hernandez. "Orthogonal gridworks loaded normally to their planes." Proc. A.S.C.E., Journal of the Structural Division, January 1960, St. 1.

Martin, J. and J. Hernandez. "General solution of space frameworks." Proc. A.S.C.E., Journal of the Structural Division, August 1961, pp. 47–73.

Massachusetts Institute of Technology, Department of Civil Engineering. *Stress. A Users' Manual.* The M.I.T. Press, Cambridge, Mass., 1964.

Matheson, J. L. "Moment distribution applied to rectangular rigid space frame." *Journal of I.C.E.,* No. 3, 1947–48.

Marks, R. W. *The Dymaxion World of Buckminster Fuller.* Reinhold Publishing Co., New York, 1960.

Mayor, B. *Introduction a la statique graphique des systèmes de l'espace.* Payot & Co., Lausanne, 1926.

McGloughlin, S. "The design and construction of simple space frames for roofs." *Civil Engineering and Public Works Review,* April, 1953.

McHale, J. "Richard Buckminster Fuller." *Architectural Design,* July 1961, pp. 290–322.

McHale, J. "Richard Buckminster Fuller." *Makers of Contemporary Architecture.* George Braziller, New York, 1962.

Mengeringhausen, M. "Die Mero-Buweise." 1. Auflage, Berlin 1942. 2. Auflage, Berlin, 1944.

Michalds, J., and B. Grossfield. "Analysis of interconnected space frames." I.A.B.S.E., 5 Congress Rio De Janeiro, 1964, p. 275.

Nashlund, Kenneth C. "Design Considerations for Horizontal Space Frames." *Architectural Record,* August 1964, pp. 152–155.

Nilson, A. H. "Folded plate structures of light gauge steel." Journal of the Structural Division. Proc. A.S.C.E., October 1961, pp. 215–237.

Organization for European Economic Cooperation. "Cost Savings Through Standardization, Simplification, Specialization in the Building Industry." Paris, December 1954.

Organization for European Economic Cooperation. "Modular Coordination in Building," Project No. 174, Paris, August 1956.

Organization for European Economic Cooperation. "Prefabricated Building —A Survey of Some European Systems." Project No. 226, Paris, December 1958.

Pandya, A. H. and R. J. Fowler. "The all-welded diagonal grid applied to plane and spatial structures." Arc welding, in Design, Manufacture and Construction, Section V, Chapter I. J. F. Lincoln Arc Welding Foundation, March 1939.

Perry, D. J. Aircraft Structures. McGraw-Hill Book Co., Inc. 1949, pp. 32–36.

Pippard, A. J. S. "Stress analysis for space frames." Civil Engineering, December, 1935.

Poniz, D. "Structural forms in geometry, plastic art and architecture." Projekt, No. 1 (15), 1959.

Proceedings of the International Conference on Space Structures, to be published by Blackwell Scientific Publications, Ltd., London, 1967–1968.

Ramirez, R. A. "Load analysis of hexagonal grids." M.Sc. Thesis, University of London, 1959.

Rapp, E. R. "Space structures in steel." Architectural Record, November 1961, pp. 190–194.

Rawlings, B. "The general moment distribution analysis of space frames." The Structural Engineer, June 1960.

Richards, J. D. "Stress-determination for a three-dimensional rigid-jointed framework by the method systematic relaxation of constraints." Journal of I.C.E., Vol. 1936–1937.

Le Ricolais, R. "Grids and space frames—an investigation on structures." A graduate report. University of Michigan.

Le Ricolais, R. "30 ans de recherches sur les structures." L'architecture d'aujourd'hui, No. 108, June–July 1963.

Le Ricolais, R. "Essai sur des systèmes réticulés à 3 dimensions." Aribles des Ponts et Chaussies, July, 1940.

Robak, D. "Structural applications of plastics in double-layer space grids." Paper No. K3. International Conference on Space Structures, London, 1966.

Roxbee, Cox H. "A two-dimensional approach to three-dimensional framework problems," Journal of the London Mathematical Society, Vol. 18, 1943.

Samuely, F. "Space frames and stressed skin construction." Civil Engineering and Public Works Review, Vol. 47, No. 553, July 1952, pp. 564–566, No. 554, August 1952, pp. 655–657.

Sbarounis, J. A. and M. P. Gaus. "Analysis of a two-way truss system." Journal of the Structural Division, Proceedings of the American Society of Civil Engineers, Vol. 85, No. ST2, February 1959, pp. 45–69.

Schulze-Fielitz, Eckhard "Raumstrukturen." Bauwelt, No. 10, S. 262, 1961.

Schulze-Fielitz, Eckhard "Une Theorie de l'occupation de l'espace." L'architecture d'aujord'hui, No. 102, June-July 1962.

S.C.S.D. "Space grid for schools, U.S.A. Systems Building." Interbuild, October 1965.

Siegel, Curt. Structure and Form in Modern Architecture. Reinhold Publishing Corp., New York, 1962.

Soare, M. "Hub speeds space frame erection." Engineering News Record, Vol. 172, No. 121, May 21, 1964.

Southwell, R. V. "Primary stress determination in space frames." Engineering, 1920, p. 6.

Southwell, R. V. "On the calculation of stresses in braced frameworks." Proceedings of the Royal Society, series A, Vol. 139, No. A 839, p. 475.

Steinhaus, Hugo. Mathematical Snapshots. Oxford University Press, New York, 1960.

Stuart, Duncan. "Polyhedral and mosaic transformations." Student publications of the School of Design, North Carolina State, of the University of North Carolina at Raleigh, Vol. 12, No. 1, 1963.

Suter. "Die Mero Hallen der Interbow." Acier, Stahl, Steel, No. 1, S. 1, Berlin, 1958.

Taylor, Robert J. "Space Truss Slab, Building as Systems," M.Arch. Thesis, School of Architecture and Planning, Massachusetts Institute of Technology, 1965.

Tezcan, S. S. "Computer analysis of plane and space structures." ASCE Struct. Eng. Conf. 1964, Conference Reprint No. 130.

"The tube goes to work in structure." Architectural Forum, January 1960.

"Triodetic structures." Architectural Forum, November 1963, pp. 185–192.

Unistrut Corporation. "Building With the Unistrut Space-Frame System, Technical Data and Design Guide." Wayne, Mich., Atwood Development Co., 1959.

Unistrut Corporation. "Unistrut System of Construction 2, Hoover Elementary School, Wayne, Mich., Atwood Development Co., Design Brochure No. 2, 1956.

Unistrut Corporation. "Unistrut System of Construction 3, Factory for Unistrut of Canada, Ltd., Chatham, Canada." Wayne, Mich., Atwood Development Co. Design Brochure No. 3, 1957.

Unistrut Corporation. "Unistrut System of Construction 4, Hubbard Street School, Wayne, Michigan." Wayne, Mich., Design Brochure No. 4, 1957.

Unistrut Corporation. "Unistrut System of Construction 5, Sheldon School, Wayne, Michigan." Wayne, Mich., Design Brochure No. 5, 1958.

Unistrut Corporation. "A Unistrut Demountable Building Package 6, Trade Fair Pavilions—U.S. Department of Commerce." Wayne, Mich., Design Brochure No. 6, 1959.

Unistrut Corporation. "Unistrut System of Construction 7, Ann Arbor Gymkhana, Ann Arbor, Michigan." Wayne, Mich., Design Brochure No. 7, 1959.

Unistrut Corporation. "Unistrut System of Construction 8, Jacee Park Pavilion, Wayne, Michigan." Wayne, Mich., Design Brochure No. 8, 1959.

Wachsmann, K. The Turning Point of Building. Reinhold Publishing Corp., New York, 1961.

Wachsmann, K. "Group study and industrial architecture." Bauen and Wohnen, October, 1960, pp. 351–394.

Wagner, H. "The analysis of aircraft structures as space frameworks." NACA TM, 522, 1929.

Walters, Rodger and Ralph Iredale. "The Nenk method of building." RIBA Royal Institute of British Architects Journal, June 1964, pp. 259–274.

Wayne, T. "Engineering problems of an all welded two-way truss system." Welding Journal, June 1958, pp. 565–569.

Welton, Beckett and Associates. "Space frames cost less than $4.00 a square foot." Architectural Record. March 1966.

Wright, D. T. "Space Frames," RAIC/L'IRAC Journal, June 1964.

Yoshinari, Takeshi. Isao Nakamara, and Stsuro Suzaki. "Gymnasium in Ube." Bauen and Wohnen, July 1960, pp. 244–249.